Mindset Reimagined

An Invitation to Personal Disruption
and Reinvention

by Charlene Dark

Mindset Reimagined:
An Invitation to Personal Disruption and Reinvention

Copyright © Charlene Dark (2025)

ISBN Paperback: 979-8-89576-122-9
ISBN Hardback: 979-8-89576-123-6

Published by:

Dedication

To those in my life who have influenced and encouraged me to share my ideas with the world.

Table of Contents

Introduction

You've probably seen the large selection of leadership and self-help books online and in bookstores. There aren't just shelves full of them – they have their own entire, ever-expanding section. Some people claim that over 4 billion leadership books are written each year. Among my favorites are those authored by names I'm sure you're familiar with: Simon Sinek, Tony Robbins, Jim Collins, and Patrick Lencioni.

I highly recommend books by these and other authors, but my first recommendation is this one – and not just because I wrote it. This is not another book about how to become a great leader or a better person. It's about disruption and reinvention, specifically of yourself. *This* is the book I want you to read before you pick up *The Motive, Start with Why, Good to Great,* or *Awaken the Giant Within.* When you've read this book, you'll be ready for those others.

Let me explain: I used to race cars for fun. It would have been a huge mistake for me to have started with a NASCAR race-ready vehicle with the idea of just flooring it and going as fast as possible around the track. I doubt I would have gone very far. I had to prepare, and this is what this book is intended to do – prepare you. Instead of taking a huge leap into the unknown, I'll show you how to effect profound change in your life by taking one step at a time, sometimes employing micro modifications, other times committing to a behavioral transformation that will take time and effort. And I promise you – it will be life-changing.

I have one overriding purpose that has followed me all my life: I want to help. I want to make a difference. I want to make life better for everyone I touch.

Perhaps that's because I had a rough childhood and often thought I might write about how I came through it and how I feel so blessed to be where I am today, the CEO of my own successful advisory services company and COO of a global services provider in the MedTech industry. However, no matter which road I was walking or how rough the footing was, I always wanted people to benefit and hopefully learn from my experiences.

So, I chewed on this idea of writing a book for some time before putting virtual pen to paper. Should it be fiction? Non-fiction? Biographical? As my career thrived and people consistently told me I was a great leader, I began to reflect on their words. I didn't feel particularly special, but clearly, I was having a positive impact on many people.

What was my secret sauce? And if I found the recipe, how could I bottle it and pay it forward? I have an analytical mind and wanted good, solid answers to those questions. It turned out that the ingredients to the recipe were the simplest things we were taught as children: common courtesy, kindness, honesty, and tolerance. I sat with those thoughts for a while and came to the conclusion that the book I wanted to write was non-fiction and based on biographical experiences. Putting my thoughts to paper went on my bucket list – but not at the top. The universe and fate had a different plan.

In mid-July 2024, at 2 p.m. on a Sunday, I was sitting in the departure lounge of the RDU International Airport, waiting to board a delayed flight to Chicago. Beside me was a young woman who introduced herself as Monique, and who told me she had recently been promoted to a managerial position within her company. She was anxious because suddenly, she was going to be managing her peers. How would she handle it?

When she asked me what work I did, I said I was in operational strategy and leadership development, and I was on my way to meet with a client for an intensive mentoring session.

"Can you tell me more about it?" she asked.

"There is a simplicity to what I do," I said. "To create trust in people, you don't want to be somebody you're not. You start with a conversation, and you put yourself in their shoes. It's the biggest piece of advice I can give – whenever you're having a conversation, always remember what you sound like and how you're delivering your words."

"What should I do in my position?" she asked.

"When you're giving a person advice, first make sure you've asked if they're open to it. Once invited, think about where they're at and why they're asking, and address the situation head-on," I said. "But do so in a way that doesn't come across as arrogant, and at the same time, doesn't come across as passive or evasive. You have to find that dynamic balance – 'These are the facts, and this is how I see us working together.' It starts with a fact-based conversation anchored in respectful delivery."

She took that in and asked, "Have you written a book?"

I thought about the bucket list item. "I'd really like to write a book," I replied. "I probably should do it sooner rather than later."

"Well, if you ever do, please let me know because I'll buy it."

I gave the conversation no more thought, but Monique was now implanted in my memory.

Twenty-four hours later, I was in the greater Milwaukee area with my mentee, John, digging into the issues that were blocking him from realizing his full leadership potential. We were pulling apart his communication style. How were his conversations going? Were they good conversations? Were they working? Was he getting the results he was aiming for? So much to unpack – or so we thought.

During the session, John looked at me. "You should write a book."

"Funny," I said. "A young lady said the same thing to me twenty-four hours ago."

"That's a sign," he said.

The next morning, my husband called me at my hotel. "Your check came."

Oh.

I had received an inheritance from a relative I never knew – one of those "impossible" things people dream about but that never happens in real life. Except it did, and the amount was enough that I could stop working for six months to write a book if I wanted to.

Twenty minutes later, a good friend, Linda, called. I told her about the recent events and she volunteered the fact that her husband was an editor and would be happy to help me.

Well.

Those were a lot of signs in a small window of time. Perhaps I needed to explore this book-writing thing again.

Back home, I searched the internet for any information I could find about how to write a book. What preparations did I have to make? Was there an outline or formula to follow? How would I get it out there? And then I had a thought: *Stephen King lives across the key from our house in Florida. Maybe I should just knock on his door.*

Maybe not.

A couple of weeks passed while I dug into other, more urgent tasks. Then, while scrolling through my LinkedIn messages, I saw one from Audrey Her with *Authors on Mission*: "Have you ever thought about writing a book?"

How many more notes from the universe did I need?

I was skeptical. In fact, being skeptical is my default position, and as an aside, if you are a skeptic and you've read this far, I know how you feel. I have decades of crossed arms and raised eyebrows under my proverbial belt.

I decided to talk to Audrey, not to take her up on any sort of offer (I should be able to do this myself), but to find out how she knew I'd been thinking about becoming an author. Was my computer listening to me? I wanted facts. I always want facts.

"I don't think I'm interested in your services," I said. "But this is just too coincidental."

"I didn't send that message to you," she said. "One of my team members did. We don't use artificial intelligence. My team scrolls through LinkedIn profiles looking for people who we think would be a good fit for our company and who have a compelling story to tell."

We talked for ninety minutes. Her transparency and honesty satisfied my inner seasoned skeptic as she walked me through her company's writing and publishing process. I was convinced.

I had never written a book, and if I wanted the highest probability of creating the best vehicle for my message to reach the greatest number of people, which would meet my goal of helping people, I needed a professional to do that. I've always told people I don't color my own hair for a reason: I'm not a professional, and the probability my hair will come out puce is pretty high.

And so, thanks to Monique, John, and other nudges along the way, I wrote this book.

I want to convey a simple message. I invite us all to take a breath and pause and allow space for a variety of opinions and beliefs to coexist in the world. I want us to celebrate our differences. We don't have to settle into a narrow focus that shuts out those who are not like us. If we could approach every conversation with the intent to understand rather than attack, we would have a better world.

Yes, we have issues – mental, physiological, biological, and neurological – but that isn't a reason for the hate I see in the world today. I want us to be proud of who we are, proud of our values, and tolerant of others who are different.

I've been on this journey all my life. I accelerated it in 2004 when I participated in the Landmark Forum, a personal development program. I went in as a skeptic. I'm still a skeptic; that didn't change. What changed was a deep understanding of what made me tick, who I wanted to be, and what I needed to do to achieve the life and relationships I wanted.

It's not hyperbole to say that a weekend in 2004 changed my life. There was a "shift" in my mind. I developed the tools I needed to be compassionate, understanding, and discerning. What I learned stuck with me. Not everyone has the profound experience I had, just as not everyone is deeply moved by any program available or by any of the wonderful books available online or in stores.

I was ready. I'd been taking steps all my life that had prepared me for a deep and meaningful transformation. I wrote earlier that this book is about taking the steps that will prepare you for a genuine awakening. I want this book to be your inspiration for making a shift in your life.

Those other great books will tell you *how* to achieve success. They'll give you the frameworks, techniques, tools, and steps to achieving what you want. But before you can start on the "doing" part of life, you have to master the "being" part. In our society today, we are of the mindset that we have to have something (money, car, fame) to do what we want to do, which will allow us to be happy and fulfilled.

The correct order is to **be** (who you are), and you will **do** what is in line with your purpose. Then you will have joy, happiness, and fulfillment.

This book is about addressing the art of being. If you're a leader *acting* like you *think* a leader should behave, tossing aside humility and vulnerability, you won't be as effective as you could be. You have to show up authentically, and that applies to all our relationships, even the ones we may think don't especially matter.

I hope that through my words and storytelling, you will see the benefit of shifting your mindset and making micro-changes in your actions that will help you flourish. When you make that shift and implement those changes, you'll find your anxiety dropping away. Why? Because when you shift to being true to who you are, you'll no longer have to worry about keeping up a front or being who others expect you to be. There is a measure of peace in letting go and just being you.

There may be days when you're not in a good space, but when you've shifted your mindset, you can let that go. It's about being cognizant and striving every day for congruence between who you are and your actions.

You've already read that I advocate micro changes. I want you to drive a go-kart before you take on NASCAR. Making a small change will stop you from being overwhelmed and walking away. More importantly, determining the "best" thing on which to focus makes a big difference in the overall shift. I like to focus on one thing. That one change will send out ripples like a rock tossed into a pond. The bigger the issue—or rock—the larger the ripples, or solutions.

I hope this book is a large rock that sends out ripples as far as possible. If you learn something and it enhances your life, I invite you to pay it forward. Tell your friends, and I hope they'll tell their friends, who'll tell their friends. Together, we will create a better world.

Chapter 1

Being Authentic

"Be the person others want to emulate."

Before you have a conversation, before you give some tough feedback, and before you begin a relationship, you have to come from a place of being authentic.

"Authenticity" has become a buzzword in today's leadership and self-improvement speak, but what does it actually mean? *Merriam-Webster* defines it as "genuine, bona fide, being actually and exactly what is claimed. Authentic implies being fully trustworthy in accordance with fact."

Psychology Today has this to say: "Authenticity is acting according to one's true self and behaving congruently with values and personality."

When I contemplate being authentic, I think of being real and open, but both those words beg to be defined as well. Authenticity is a way of *being*, and there is an associated feeling with being authentic. We know when we are in the presence of a person who has no masks or barriers, no image, and no pretensions. They have an inexplicable aura that draws you in. You want to be around them because they leave you feeling better. If you were to ask me if I'm authentic, I'd like to be able to say, "Yes, one hundred percent of the time." That would be a lie. But do I strive to be? Yes. I do my best to show up as the person I know I am – a real and sometimes raw human being.

I want people to trust that I will be honest and transparent in my communication, interactions, and relationships with them. I want them to trust that I have room for their opinions and that I will try to understand their viewpoints. I also want them to understand that I may not share their views and opinions – and that's okay.

I won't be "on it" every day. I won't always present the best version of myself, and this is also perfectly okay. There will be days when I am unmotivated and I may even be downright unpleasant, but being authentic means I'll give myself the space and grace to be in that mindset, and I'll use the skills and strengths I have to persevere through those times to once again be congruent with what I know is the best version of myself.

During a recent dinner with two close friends, one of them asked a question pertaining to networking.

"How often do you reach out to people in your network?" she asked.

Immediately, almost reactively, I responded, "Define *often*."

"Good point," she said, and we moved on to a different topic.

Driving home, I found myself thinking about that brief part of the larger conversation – I was bothered and, frankly, a bit disappointed in myself. Instead of giving her a thoughtful answer, I'd mirrored the question back to her. Not acceptable.

The next morning, I called her to apologize. She sounded puzzled. "Apologize for what?"

"I didn't answer your question," I said." And you deserve better than that."

"I didn't even notice," she said.

"But you deserve better," I insisted. The point was that I had to "clean up" the interaction. I had not given my friend the best version of me. Cleaning up wasn't just for my friend's sake. More importantly, it was about my integrity and about always striving to be the best me I can be – for myself and those around me.

People often tell me, "When I leave a conversation with you, I don't have to question where I stand with you." A prospective client recently told me that she really appreciated my directness. I pride myself on that because I believe it's essential to be authentic in our communications in such a way that we maintain a high level of respect and dignity in our interactions.

I aim for a strong overlap between who I am and who you think I am – ideally, they would coincide completely. But part of being authentic is the ability to be honest with yourself. You have to know yourself and be willing to truthfully examine and acknowledge the less-than-ideal aspects of who you are.

Look into yourself and be honest about what you find. If you find yourself in a foul mood with people during less-than-stellar conditions, that probably means you're human. We're all perfectly flawed. Embrace those aspects of yourself, recognize the impact you can have when you're not projecting your "best self," and take action to recalibrate back to center. The person receiving your words is a human being with feelings and thoughts worthy of respect. If you happen to miss the recalibration moment in real time, go back and clean it up (as I did with my friend).

People sometimes misuse the concept of authenticity as a shield for being mean and disrespectful. No! Authenticity goes hand-in-hand with compassion and caring about others. If you don't care about being the *best* you, this book is not for you. If you're rude and self-serving and you think authenticity is saying, "That's just the way I am," you won't find anything here of value to you. Authenticity is never an excuse for bad behavior.

I have a friend who wears her authenticity like an inside-out coat. She calls it authenticity. I believe her dismissive, "This is just who I am" attitude is actually shielding her authenticity. I know there is an amazing version of her deep inside; I wish she would spend more time in that space and adjust her mindset to be less judgmental. If you've been hurt and are afraid of being vulnerable and open, then you may have developed protective armor. Taking it off and letting your guard down is no easy thing, but what lies underneath is the real you, and only the genuine you can lead a rich, fulfilling life.

I believe we have a good sense of our own authenticity. We know the moment we put our coat on inside-out, and when we turn it right side in again. I also think we have a good sense of when another person is being genuine with us. When we connect with people, we are connecting with the real deal – we can't be intimate with a mask.

I know that whether I'm interviewing a candidate for a job or meeting someone at a party, I have a sense of their authenticity that can't readily be explained. I suspect we all have that sixth sense to some degree. You've probably run into people who try too hard to make an impression, or who have something to hide, or who are trying to make the "right" connections.

However, authenticity isn't just about what we do or say. The heart of it is our thoughts. Are all my thoughts—or anyone's—always congruent with who we are or aspire to be? Of course not, but incongruent thoughts are countered by thoughts that are in alignment with our authentic selves. Staying alert to this incongruence and taking deliberate steps to course-correct will take time and a great deal of effort. Remember, mindset reset is not a switch-flipping exercise. It's a marathon, not a sprint.

My client, John, will occasionally express ideas or thoughts negatively. "It's been a real struggle today."

My advice to him is, "John, you need to flip it."

"I've had lots of opportunities today." And just like that, he has put the issues of the day in a different light.

When you "flip it," you're not only using different words; you're changing how you are thinking about the situation. I'm not saying it's always going to be easy, but the effort is worth it. The "flipped" thoughts that are in alignment with who we are bring out the best version of us, and the best version is our authenticity.

One of my older grandchildren, who is nineteen as I write this, is one of the most authentic people I know. When he was a young child, he was, to use a gross understatement, rambunctious. Of our oldest daughter's four children (I'm her bonus mom), he was the one my husband and I were concerned would make front-page headlines – and not in a good way! He managed to stay off the media's radar because our daughter raised her children with discipline and respect. Today, people are drawn to him for his caring nature, his ability to make good choices, his talent for participating in conversations with persons of any age, and his sensitivity to others. He is one of those people who carry that aura. He doesn't *act* like he cares – he genuinely does care. He restores my hope that the younger generation will create a compassionate society. I'm very happy to say I have a granddaughter who is following in my grandson's footsteps, establishing an identity that is steeped in authenticity.

One of the simplest ways we know whether we have interacted with an authentic person or someone who is wearing a mask is how we feel after the interaction. Do you come away feeling better, or do you feel like you need to take a shower?

When I am interacting with someone, I can tell if they're interested in me, in themselves, or in us. My grandson is perpetually interested in "us."

When people walk away from me after we've talked, I want them to feel as good or better than when we began. That's what I look for in interactions. If I feel as good or better, that's a measure of their authenticity. That doesn't mean I expect you to be on top of your game at all times, but I want you to be clear on who you are, including your strengths, your fears, your inadequacies, and your insecurities.

If I'm in a conversation and find myself questioning or judging or becoming increasingly skeptical, I will step back and examine what is going on. Do they want something from me, and they're not asking for it directly? Do they want to get close to me because they believe there's something in it for them?

I have a friend whom I love dearly, and it breaks my heart to watch him chase after status. I wish he could realize that status and fame aren't real. What void is he trying to fill with those intangible constructs? Why can't he see the beauty of the genuine person I've experienced and choose to spend more time in that space?

I have my own stories of being less than real. At the dinner I was having with my former employees and friends, I shared an unflattering story from my past. Why did I do that? I suppose I wanted them to see the whole me, not just the "good" persona. I never want people to put me on a pedestal.

My friend, Marianne, listened to my story and said, "All these experiences have made you who you are today." A simple yet profound statement.

She was right. I have made bad choices. Apparently, at the time I made them, I thought they were good ideas. And I'll continue to make a few bad choices as I go through life. We inevitably do. Good people sometimes make bad choices, but bad choices do not necessarily define our character.

Being authentic doesn't mean you're always at your best – it's being all of who you are. Authenticity is unapologetically being a perfectly flawed human being and having the ongoing desire to stay in a state of congruence between your "being" and your "doing."

It can be easy to put on our cloak or armor instead of confronting the things we don't want to look at or show to others. Maybe we put up barriers because we don't have enough confidence or belief in ourselves – that we are lovable because of all that we are, not despite who we are. However, kindness, courtesy, compassion, and tolerance shine through when we drop our defenses.

I'll say again: you have to know who you are. The search for self is a quest worth following. Are you a petty, angry, gossipy person? No, you're not. That's your trauma speaking. You're caring, compassionate, smart, and kind. You want to help people.

The question you need to ask when you're not at your best is, "Why am I behaving in ways that are incongruent with who I know I am or who I'm striving to become?"

You're not perfect, but to be you, you have to take off the mask and be unapologetic for being imperfect. Getting to that place may not be an easy journey, but it's possible. If I can do it, I know you can. I had to be okay with the ongoing battle with my inner voice suggesting I wasn't worthy and not good enough. I still work on it every day. And I know I *am* worthy, and I *am* good enough.

One of the people I coach recently told me, "I have imposter syndrome, and my former coach said we'd get rid of it."

I said, "It will never go away. That's part of who you are – an instilled, innate way of thinking. We won't eliminate it, but you'll learn how to behave around it."

We all have a *not-best version of myself* column opposite our *best version of ourselves* column. In the first column are the things that trigger behaviors incongruent with your being. When you get on those behaviors, I'll offer suggestions on how to "get off" them. You become a master when you "get off" those behaviors before anyone realizes you even "got on" them.

I have plenty of things in column number one, like being impatient and quick to judge. I walked into the living room the other day and glanced at an ad that was playing. Instantly, I thought, "Well, how stupid is that." And then, seconds later, "Who am I to judge, and why do I care?"

That's the act of a master. I had a judgmental thought, recognized it, and course-corrected. My first thought was incongruent with who

I am. It takes time to master course correction. It also takes time to achieve congruence. The effort you put in will pay off more than you can imagine. You will accumulate a wealth of beautiful relationships. Perhaps even more importantly, you will feel free and genuinely "you" inside your skin.

The foundation of authenticity creates a mindset that allows you to listen to others' opinions and make choices based on your truth and how you want to proceed.

Being authentic doesn't automatically lead to good communication, but it's the solid foundation for that to take place. Your authenticity drives your mindset. If I'm wearing a mask, I've already put up a barrier to being completely open, and my mindset is not accessible to possibility, not only to what the other person has to say but to see my own shortcomings in my interactions.

CHAPTER 2

Mindset

"Being is an active, deliberate state that is ongoing."

The American Psychological Association defines mindset as "a state of mind that influences how people think about and then enact their goal-directed activities in ways that may systematically promote or interfere with optimal functioning."

The website, verywellmind, with a board consisting of mental health professionals, defines mindset as "a set of beliefs that shape how you make sense of the world and yourself. It influences how you think, feel, and behave in any given situation. It means that what you believe about yourself impacts your success or failure."

I see mindset as a space open to receiving information and being open to looking at it objectively. Even when the information is counter to what I expected or wanted, I would make every effort not to reject it but to look at it without immediate prejudice. My bias will certainly be working in the background, but this clear space allows me to pause and acknowledge the possibility of another viewpoint. Perhaps my view of an issue could change based on information I didn't previously have.

How do we attain this mindset in a world that is becoming increasingly polarized, broken up into warring tribes, and demanding unwavering allegiance to one particular worldview? Forty years ago, we had a fraction of the input we have today. Our ability to be open has become damaged and impaired by this constant barrage we absorb daily through our devices and all forms of media – many of which offer no evidence of facts or data behind the information they publish.

Compounding this problem is that the amount of information we get from newspapers, television, podcasts, social media, radio, and influencers on YouTube and TikTok is far from reliable. We've shifted from facts and evidence to opinion.

In September 2020, the documentary *The Social Dilemma* saw tech experts from Silicon Valley sounding the alarm on the dangerous impact of social networking, which Big Tech uses in an attempt to manipulate and influence. CNN reported on research that showed that twenty-five percent of information on Facebook is false, while another study found that from August 2020 to January 2021, misinformation received six times more clicks on Facebook than posts containing factual news.

Those statistics are frightening. And it's not just the internet. TV channels claiming to be news simply spew opinions to their viewers, or present one particular point of view meant to reinforce what its audience already believes, or convince the "nonbelievers" to convert.

Opening your mind makes you vulnerable. What if you discover that some of the beliefs you've held, possibly for years, are suddenly being challenged – by you? Many people are simply not interested in going down that road.

Sticking with the views you already have is safe and comfortable. And if you share those views with a group you are emotionally attached to, it becomes even more difficult to open the door to other possibilities. That's the basis of cults, and it's also the reason so many people today are defending their views with such passion, and even in some cases, violence.

Remember, facts are not truth. Despite Kellyanne Conway's assertion during a *Meet the Press* interview on January 22, 2017, "alternative facts" are not facts. They may be her truth, but a fact is data-driven, and it stands on its own merits.

If you want a clear and open mindset, it's worth your time to go after the facts. I'm a strategic advisor to a startup that is doing remarkable work on privacy technology. That spurred me to look at data breaches, and what I found was mind-boggling. The U.S. government's health and human services website lists healthcare-focused companies that had a data breach in the past twenty-four months and are under investigation. The list was one hundred pages long with about fifty rows per page! The information I had before my investigation was that these data breaches happened, but I had not expected this extent. I got the facts, and now I am curious to search out the facts about other sectors that have had data breaches.

Trusted sources also make mistakes. Legitimate media will quickly print a retraction. Mistakes happen. It's up to us to discern whether misinformation is a genuine error or intentional. It's not a Sisyphean task. It simply means you have to be discerning and, more importantly, willing to know the facts. Sources like Snopes.com are useful. We'll talk in-depth about skepticism in the next chapter, but briefly, healthy skepticism today is a great defense against false information. Let your evidence for or against an issue be based on reality as opposed to "Joe said so," or even more commonly, "I read it on the internet."

One insidious side-effect of our increasingly polarized politics is people taking words out of context. And it's not just politics. The inclination to listen to others, with the idea of finding something to "use against them," is increasing. We are human, we make mistakes. Sometimes, we say something we wish we could take back. The "gotcha" mindset is the opposite of the one we need to cultivate. The struggle to be open is real, and it feels less safe every day.

However, if we want to do better, we have to try, and if we are always doing the best we can given what we know, then one of the secrets to doing better is to know more. My niece has said to me for years that I'm addicted to learning. She's right. I listen to others, often in order to learn, but I also trust my HS (healthy skepticism) meter. It allows me to take in what I hear without necessarily believing it at face value. However—and this is important—I don't necessarily discount what I hear.

When I respond to someone with the statement, "I get it," it doesn't necessarily mean I agree with them or that I view the issue the same way. When I listen to them, I want to understand. Since joining the medtech services company, I have witnessed several situations where business decisions were made that I didn't agree with. Our investors are making key decisions on investments, including how much, when, and how to spend the investments, and their choices are influenced, not dictated, by reports from our executive team. The final choices are based on a myriad of factors including risk and the business needs, which are sometimes in conflict. While I may not agree with the outcomes of the annual plan and the allocated funds, I understand the position the team is in and respect the choices they make. I get it. Getting to the place where you can truly "get it" despite the doubts you may have about the situation, choices, or directions somehow removes those negative feelings when you don't get your way.

Given the challenge of adopting an open mindset, how do you do it? You choose to. I don't believe there's a specific formula or framework for that kind of shift, but if you're ready, you'll do it. If you're reading this, I'll assume you're ready. It's said that an addict will not start healing until he or she is ready. A closed mindset can be heavily addictive because there's a world of "evidence" telling you you're right to think the way you do.

If you fall back on "This is just who I am" or "This is how I was raised," you're doing yourself a tremendous disservice. You're saying you're stuck and helpless where you are. You're a victim. I believe you have the power to choose. In his book and video, *The Last Lecture,* Randy Pausch says that when *you* believe that you have the power to choose, that's when change starts.

You can choose to continue to hold on to your old paradigms, or you can shift. It's always a choice. I get that it can be hard work. Disruption and reinvention aren't easy. We're always happy to demand that others change, but we're not quite so eager to say, "Yes. Absolutely" if someone points out that maybe we need to change, transform, or even reinvent.

You always have a choice. Sometimes, the choice isn't between a walk in the sleet and rain and a trip to Hawaii. Sometimes, it's about which side of the street will keep you driest. But as Elie Wiesel so famously said, even when he was in Auschwitz and all seemed to be lost, he could always choose his attitude. Perhaps our attitude is the most fundamental choice of all.

When I was fourteen and moved away from my mother's house, I was choosing not to be a victim of my circumstances. When the opportunity for me to make that choice presented itself, I grabbed it. I could have chosen to stay, but I wanted so much more for myself. The life I live today is based on the choices I have made, starting with that one at age fourteen.

If I could go back and show my ten-year-old self the life I live today, she would think I was showing her a movie clip. Nothing I am, do, and have now was within the realm of her reality. My circumstances drove me to choose, and my choices determined my present circumstances.

To choose and decide are two different things. To decide, you let go of one option to do another. To choose is to understand all your options and select one, given the information you have. If you want to make great choices, you need great information, and it's up to you to get it. Learn. Be informed. Have a mindset that's open to possibilities.

If you have trouble making a choice, take a long look at the word "but." "But" is a roadblock that stops you from moving, and "however" is "but's first cousin. "I want to go to the party, *but* I have to write an essay." You are stuck on the proverbial horns of a dilemma. Take "but" out of the equation. Replace it. "I want to go to the party, *and* I have to write an essay." Now you have a simple choice. Either go to the party or write the essay, or is there another option? Can you do both? How?

My husband is Catholic. I'm Methodist. I support his Catholicism, and I'm not going to convert. It's a simple choice without an emotional charge. However, if I were to say, I support his Catholicism, but I'm not going to convert, the sentence takes on a different meaning. Immediately, there's an underlying note of conflict and possibly, resentment. "But" implies discord. "But" is a bag filled with negative emotions, barriers, and dividing lines.

"But" is an obstacle.

You may ask yourself why you should do the hard work of transforming your mindset. After all, you have your tribe that agrees with you about your worldview. It's pretty comfortable where you are. Changing to an open, more vulnerable mindset seems pretty risky. What are you going to get out of it?

You're going to get out of it what you choose to get out of it.

That's the power of choice.

Intellectually, you may be prepared to take on a new mindset, but as soon as someone casts the first aspersion on your political leader of choice or your favorite Muppet character, you're ready to retaliate, right? You could choose to listen to why those people who clearly don't see things the way you do came to that conclusion, and still conclude it's complete BS, or you could listen and see a point of view you had never considered. You could take your new mindset from an intellectual exercise and move it deeper. You can listen to theories of how bad things could get if … or you can let common sense and facts guide your thoughts and actions.

Let reputable sources and good data guide your thinking. The first time good, solid information bumps up against your beliefs, you have to resist the urge to say, "That's garbage." Leave room for the facts, even if they go against what you believe. Our minds don't want to change. That's why this is such hard work. No one wants to be wrong. Your mind is telling you that by changing your view or even being open to a new idea, you are admitting you were wrong. How embarrassing!

It takes practice to confront a fact that directly contradicts what you believe. What's the first thing that goes through your mind and maybe even comes out of your mouth? "Yes, but ..."

An open mindset doesn't mean you have to change your mind, it's about having all the facts and choosing your position based on that. It may be the exact position you started with, and now you know it rests on a solid foundation. I tell my business clients, "Get as much data as you can so you can make a well-informed choice. The more data you have, the better. Then, when you make your choice, you'll be comfortable, knowing you are standing on facts, evidence, and then, lastly, your opinion."

As you practice and become more adept at approaching your life and the people in it with an open mind, you'll discover subtle and profound changes. When I know I have based certain choices on facts and data, I can look at myself in the mirror and know I was fair. That's important to me. Am I still biased? Probably, but that's okay because I also listened openly and checked my facts. I was fair. If I have a truly open mindset and I am listening to learn, I will often come away from a conversation or interaction with a pivot. The degree of my pivot will vary, but when I have a position and I've been open to learning, most often, there is one, and that allows me to feel I've been fair.

More than that, I feel a sense of my own authenticity. It's a feeling that what I have done is in alignment with my integrity and sense of justice.

One of the key qualities that leads to this feeling is my relentless and thorough research into facts, and that is spurred on by my inner skeptic. We'll talk about cultivating and honoring that skeptic in the next chapter.

CHAPTER 3

The Healthy Skeptic

"It starts with me – the groundswell is up to us."

I regularly tell people I should live in Missouri, the show-me state, a moniker that stuck after Missouri Congressman Willard Duncan Vandiver in 1899 said in a speech, "I'm from Missouri, and you've got to show me," indicating he wanted clear evidence. Like the congressman, I'm a skeptic. My skepticism runs deep, but I believe I am a healthy skeptic. I'm with Ronald Reagan, who used to cite the old Russian proverb: "Trust but verify."

If not for my skepticism, I wonder if this book would have been written. When I saw the message from Audrey Her from Authors on Mission in my LinkedIn messages, I was darn skeptical. How did this woman know I was contemplating a book? Was I a victim of the algorithms buried in our search engines that had ultimately sold my information to this company?

Because I was skeptical, I chose to question her thoroughly. And because I went into the conversation with an open mindset, willing to take in new information, we talked for ninety minutes, and I thought, "Yes, this is for me." Her transparency satisfied my seasoned inner skepticism as she walked me through her company's writing and publishing process.

I had a great result, and I believe much of it was due to my healthy skepticism. But what is that? A quick Google search turns up some good definitions including these: "Healthy skepticism is being curious. The ability to know whether an explanation makes sense. Skepticism is a fundamental doctrine for any scientist that asserts nothing should be accepted nor rejected without considerable evidence." And this one, my favorite: "Healthy skepticism is a disposition that occupies the sensible space between gullibility and cynicism."

That's a great distinction because skepticism and cynicism are not the same thing. The difference is that we can be skeptical about specific information or statements; cynicism is a jaded world-view that encompasses life in general. Skepticism has its place. Combined with an open mindset, it's enlightening; if you're skeptical with a closed mindset, that's a problem.

Given today's world of AI-generated memes and misinformation that is rampant in broadcast and social media, being skeptical is a necessary skill for making informed and well-thought-out decisions.

In 1992, I was introduced to a product called Pampered Chef. The salesperson claimed I could put French fries on this amazing stone, bake them in the oven, and they would come out as crispy as if I had deep-fried them. My inner skeptic was screaming, "That can't be possible!" So I bought the stone just to prove her wrong – after making sure I could return it, of course.

Not only were the fries just as crispy, but they were even better than deep-fried, and I bought every stone Pampered Chef sold.

Healthy skepticism moved me forward because even while I was doubtful, I kept an open mind. If I'd said, "Yeah, sure," to Pampered Chef and walked away with my eyebrows still raised, I would have learned nothing. By staying open, I found a healthier way to eat French fries.

Skepticism has a reputation for being a character flaw. Not so. When someone says to me, "You're such a skeptic," they're telling me that I don't take everything at face value. My response is, "Thank you."

Trust is eroding all over the world. We've become inured to hearing pundits spin ("alternative truth," perhaps) on radio and television. We see memes pop up on social media and unthinkingly pass them along without fact-checking. We either don't believe our politicians because we know they lie, or we idolize them and follow them blindly, right or wrong. We seem to have lost the ability to think critically, and critical thinking is driven by several things, one of which is skepticism.

I mentioned in the introduction to this book that I was profoundly skeptical when I enrolled in the Landmark Forum in 2004 and that it changed my life. There was a "shift" in my mind, and I developed the tools I needed to be compassionate, understanding, and discerning. What I learned stuck with me.

I was ready to learn. I'd been taking steps all my life that had prepared me for a deep and meaningful transformation. When we arrived at the topic "What Is," the facilitator asked for a volunteer. I raised my hand. Standing in front of the room, I was asked to identify something in my life that didn't bring me joy or make me happy.

That was easy.

"My relationship with my mother."

"Who is your mother to you?" the facilitator asked.

I itemized the list: "She's not a mother. She was neglectful. She was abusive. She is a pathological liar ..." It was a long, damning recitation. I said, only half-jokingly, that I didn't think she actually wanted kids.

"Was your mother involved in anything?" the facilitator asked.

"Oh yes. She was involved in church."

"What would her fellow church-goers say about her?"

I snorted. "Huh! That she's delightful and helping, and that she's committed and engaged and cares about the community."

"What about her parents? What would they say?"

"I think they'd say that she did her best."

We talked through four or five scenarios before the facilitator asked, "So, which one is she?"

I stood very still. I looked at him. Which one was she, indeed?

At that moment, I understood the meaning of "something just is."

Sometimes, an event occurs and all the opinions, assumptions, and judgments we have about it are ours. It doesn't negate that some things are wrong or immoral, but that day, in that instant, something switched. The disdain I'd carried for my mother for so many years simply dissipated.

I wasn't suddenly flooded with a sense of love and affection, but the feelings of resentment and bitterness that I'd been hurting myself with vanished.

My mother died on June 2, 2023, after suffering a stroke two years previously. I was the child who traveled back and forth from Raleigh, North Carolina, to northeast Ohio to look after her from 2021 until she died.

Knowing my history with my mother, a friend asked me, "How can you do that after everything your mother put you through?"

"How can I not?" I replied. "I don't like her, but I love her because she's my mother. I'm her daughter, and this is the right thing to do."

"Not everyone would be as strong as you," my friend said.

No, I thought – it had nothing to do with strength. It was my mindset. She was alone, she'd had a stroke, and with the resentment gone, there was room for compassion.

If you get anything out of reading this story, I hope you see that one simple shift in mindset changed how I looked at things, and it was based on one simple question – "So, who is she?" I had to be ready for that shift. In 2004, I was ready. I'm sure that between 1980 and 2004, many people told me, "Give your mother a chance. I'm sure she did the best she could."

I was having none of that.

I wasn't ready.

When I was, and I shifted, a feeling swept over me that I'm not sure we have a word for in our language. It was a sense of genuine emotional freedom that wrapped around my soul. It wasn't intellectual, and it wasn't truly emotional either. It was something that belonged to the soul. The angst I'd been carrying unconsciously for decades disappeared. And perhaps that was the feeling – the absence of something that had been weighing me down for so very long.

I will never regret being skeptical initially when I attended a Landmark Forum introductory presentation. There are many unscrupulous and shady programs out there, but to simply remain mired in my doubt and misgivings without searching out the facts would have kept me stuck where I was in a sea of anger and resentment. Healthy skepticism allowed me to be open to possibilities, even the possibility that my mother may not have been the person my mind had conjured her to be. I'd held a truth about her that changed.

I may not be able to comprehend someone else's truth. We may be miles apart. Your truth may be that the people in that Third World country who hate Americans are evil and wrong. Others' truth might be that they are poor and desperate and are rightly angry at who they believe are their oppressors. Who am I to say who is wrong? I had to have a shift in mindset to understand that my truth is only one truth out of many possibilities. My truth matters, as does that of others. There must be room to acknowledge that facts do not equal truth. We have to understand that adding opinions to facts leads to various truths.

I only hope that children today are being taught that healthy skepticism is a quality to be nurtured. In Finland, children are being taught in primary school to discern the difference between real and "fake" news. They are learning critical thinking as soon as they can read. What a great idea!

Johann Hari's book *Stolen Focus* is sobering. When Hari's nephew was five, he loved to impersonate Elvis, who was one of his heroes. Hari was inspired to write his book when, ten years later, he took the now fifteen-year-old boy to Graceland. Like so many teens, he was not gawking at his surroundings in the Elvis mansion. Instead, he was constantly looking at his phone, endlessly scrolling, texting, and looking at his screen. Hari noticed his nephew was not alone. Every person there had their head down, staring at a phone or tablet. Visitors to Graceland are even given tablets to "guide" them through their visit!

Hari felt compelled to alert the world to what technology was doing to us. One of the reasons I love the book is that he quoted at least two people whose findings he disagreed with, but they were in the book anyway. Now, there's a man with an open mind and a desire to impart truths based on facts! By quoting those people with whom he disagreed, he also honored his readers, respecting their ability to make up their own minds.

Hari conducted meticulous research, interviewing doctors, psychologists, and tech experts. He even interviewed Aza Raskin, the man who'd invented the infinite scroll, who confessed he regretted that particular innovation and apologized for its impact on people's attention spans and the way it has been used by social media companies to keep users engaged for longer periods. For me, Hari's interpretation of his thorough research was enlightening.

Studies show that kids who are growing up with this technology are experiencing negative effects like lack of sleep, inability to focus, and mental disorders. They are also exposed to masses of misinformation, and many are unable to discern facts from lies, which heavily impacts their critical thinking abilities. These kids, and probably all of us, have to build a filter, or better yet, stage gates. The first gate asks, "Is it plausible? Does it contain even a modicum of common sense?" The second one might ask, "Is it filled with empty rhetoric, or is it fact-based? Are there stats to back this up?" And then, "Does it use emotion-packed words like *enormous, severe, tragic* – and generalities like *always* and *never*?" Instead of generalities, look for reports that include measurable data and that cite a source. With enough stage gates, you can eventually get to the truth.

I hope schools, not just in Finland, are teaching critical thinking, the close cousin to healthy skepticism. I hope the kids—and all of us—view the information we are fed critically, and if it doesn't pass through the stage gates, shut it down. Let's not be conduits for misinformation. This is not the old Clairol commercial: *don't* tell two friends.

Last of all, monitor yourself. With so much misinformation in the world, it's easy to become cynical. I don't want that for my grandchildren, but I want them to live in a fact-based world. It starts with one. If you can behave sensibly and ethically, you can pass that on. That's the groundswell.

CHAPTER 4

Intentional Communication

*"How you have conversations can have
a massive ripple effect."*

I 've been using intentional communication for many years because I want to be clear and complete in my conversations. When you've ended a communication with someone, their first response should not be, "Huh? What?"

If it is that, then you have wasted everyone's time.

The model below outlines my approach to intentional communication:

Intentional Communication
Clarity and specificity are essential to effectively and efficiently manage communications

Structuring your communication using the framework below provides the recipient clear, fact-based information on intent of communication

Why: the message should clearly articulate the reason for communication

What: provide facts/data that will help the recipient further understand the why this communication is taking place

Outline the specific ask/request: provide all necessary information to expedite the ask/request

Timeframe of response and/or requested action: it is important to be specific on when you need a response/action; don't be afraid to use bold/color

Impact: VERY IMPORTANT – the recipient needs to understand the impact of not addressing this communication and taking action to address the ask/request

What I mean by communication being complete is that people understand why this conversation is taking place, what the facts are, the supporting evidence, what you are asking for, a specific time frame for the ask, and the impact of acting or not acting.

If you're asking people to do something, they will respond better when it makes sense to them and if they understand why they are being asked to do what you're requesting. They have to be able to answer the question, "So what?" This doesn't just apply to a corporate setting.

Have you ever asked your children to clean their rooms? "Because I said so," is not a very inspiring reason, nor is it respectful. Think about trying to get your child to tidy up their space. Rather than "Go clean your room," how about, "It is my goal, and I hope the goal of the family, that we respect one another as well as the things we have worked hard for (the why). I noticed your bedroom was not even close to the most basic definition of clean when I walked by this afternoon, and the condition of your room is not how we keep our home. Your clothes are not put away or in the laundry basket, and I saw glasses and plates on the floor – none of these things are in their proper place. This mess not only makes part of the house unkept, but it is also a statement about taking pride in yourself. I expect the room to be clean before 10:00 p.m. tonight. If you cannot clean it up by then, I need you to let me know a reasonable day and time when I can expect to see a clean room. There will be no electronics for the rest of the weekend if we cannot come to a reasonable agreement for completing this task."

Here's another example that still has me shaking my head: several months ago, at my husband's company, a simple clerical error that could have been solved with a phone call and a follow-up summary blew up into a multi-departmental emergency that reached the executive level involving daily meetings consisting only of empty rhetoric and churn, not to mention a substantial investment of time and money. Intentional communication is desperately needed in situations like this, and part of "the why" is stating the problem.

When you clearly state the issue or challenge, you can get the facts and analyze them. If you miss any part of the communication framework, you are setting up the opportunity for someone to be upset or confused. Many times, a person in a state of upset or confusion is simply missing information.

One of my pet peeves is a lack of specificity. I was working with a new team one day, talking about timelines. I'm sure you've also experienced conversations that go like this:

Team member: "I'll have that to you mid-next week."

Me: "Okay – Wednesday."

Team member: "Well – um, no – let's make it Thursday."

Me: "Okay – Thursday. When on Thursday?"

Team member: "Midday."

Me: "Okay – noon."

Team member: "Um – why don't we say end of day?"

I've actually arrived at the point just before where I ask which time zone we're talking about.

That level of specificity not only sets my expectations but also instills a level of accountability. If I tell you I will have a report completed by 5 p.m. on Thursday, I have committed to deliver it. To me, ASAP stands for "as slow as possible" and goes to the bottom of the priority list.

Intentional communication delivers a level of clarity to both parties in the conversation. Nothing is left to interpretation.

Intentional communication allows both the person delivering the message and the person receiving the message to feel a sense of productivity or efficiency because when you ask me to complete a report by Friday, I have the power to say, "I'm traveling on Friday and have personal commitments over the weekend. Can we agree on the following Wednesday at 9 a.m.?" If I don't set the expectation, and simply agree to the demand, I'm going to be stressed and won't be in the right mindset to be fully present in what I'm doing. I won't give my best to the job, and I put the personal commitments I've made at risk.

The idea of intentional communication is so simple that you have to wonder why everyone isn't simply doing it, and why don't I just end this chapter right now? We all get it, right? However, most of us are not doing it, and why not?

One reason, I think, is the advent of technology, one of the greatest joys of our modern age while also being one of the worst things that's been handed to us (in my opinion, of course). While we've accelerated our ability to receive information, we've also put ourselves in a position to receive too much, both in quantity and duration and sometimes a combination of both. That's when we become overwhelmed, and when we do, we lose the mindset that's holding us in a place of strength and calm. Even the strongest people will fall over if they are bombarded relentlessly with too much information.

We all know the old saying, "A man is only as good as his word." The foundation of keeping your word is being fully aware of the commitments you are making. If you say you will do something, *know* you can deliver. That may require negotiation, and it's worth it if you want to make good on your word. The surest way to build trust is to do what you say you will. And if you can't follow through on your promise, you'd better be meticulous about cleaning it up.

The intentional communication model at the beginning of this chapter puts structure in place for how you interact with people. If I want to be the best version of myself, and if I want to honor myself and others, this model is a tool that will help me achieve that.

You may tell me that Wednesday morning is too late for the report. You need it Tuesday afternoon at the latest. And I may say, "You know, I'll have some time on the plane. I can fit it in and agree to Tuesday, end of business."

Intentional communication opens up genuine negotiations because it requires honesty, not only with the person you are communicating with but also with yourself. You can come to an alignment and solve a potential problem with an attitude of creating a win-win situation.

You may not get your ideal solution, but if your voice was heard, you have experienced a win. It's crucial that your voice be heard and that you listen to the voices of others.

In a recent coaching session with my client, John, he told me, "I'm in a place now where I have space in my day to focus on my team, on our succession, and our bigger impact – and I don't know how to behave in this space."

John was saying that he'd stepped out of his comfort zone, so of course, it was uncomfortable for him until he fully inhabited this new place. He got there by fully embracing intentional communication. Increased delegation goes hand in hand with that.

Not every conversation demands intentional communication. Employing the intentional communication model is best used when you have determined you have a specific ask and a good reason for asking.

Have you ever asked your partner to fix a leaky faucet or a warped door frame? And has your partner said, "Sure, I'll get around to it." And they don't?

First, ask yourself if a full-blown intentional communication model is even needed - you can tell them why you need it fixed. Is the reason obvious enough that you need to provide evidence that you need it fixed? What's the impact if we don't fix it? Is the energy and effort to establish an intentional communication warranted, or, do you hire someone to do it? Is it even important enough for you to spend the time, energy, and money on it? Maybe not.

When my husband and I bought our house ten years ago, we had ceiling fans in every imaginable finish: chrome, brushed bronze, brass, white – you name it, we had it. Ten years ago, I was determined to replace the fans, and for great reasons. At least, I thought they were great. I wanted all of the finishes to match and fit with my decor. It's ten years later, and guess what? I still have the same fans. Ultimately, replacing them just wasn't important enough.

I know people like to build "float" into their time requests on the assumption something will happen that will result in running late. I like to ask people, "Do you really need that? Do you want it just for your comfort?" Be honest about the time you need – and not just extra time. If you're asking someone to produce something in twenty-four hours, know *why* you need it in the turnaround period. Intentional communication allows you to be reasonable and honest. It also encompasses *how* you ask – the delivery. We'll address that next.

CHAPTER 5

What Did You Say?

"The foundation of any conversation is respect."

I t's not just what you say, it's also how you say it. Never underestimate the power of delivery.

In my twenties, I participated in a sales training seminar for a recruiting firm I had just joined. The facilitator told us a story about how she'd had to fire an employee. The message had been a tough one to deliver, but she explained how she'd approached it, the words and facts she'd used, and how she'd delivered it. When she'd completed the conversation, the employee thanked her. That anecdote and its lesson stuck with me, and it's been one that I've applied ever since.

I leaned on it a few years ago when an employee presented me with an idea to innovate and improve efficiency in key tasks. As we discussed the details and intended goals, I became less and less comfortable with how they planned to roll out the changes to the department. "I don't agree with this," I said. "If I was standing in your shoes, I would consider these certain factors and this alternate approach."

"I hear you," they said. "And I believe that the way I want to do it will work. Do you trust me?"

"Yes, I trust you," I said. "And I need to clearly convey that I see high risk in your approach, with which I am not in agreement. Because this department is yours and you are accountable for the delivery and profitability, I need to ask you, is it a risk you want to take? More than that, you're putting your job on the line for this. Are you willing to do that? That's how big a risk this is. We could potentially lose a substantial amount of money and client confidence."

They said that, yes, they were willing to take that risk.

It's important to note that we had built mutual respect and trust that allowed us to have a conversation that included conflict without risking the integrity of our relationship.

They went ahead and carried out their idea with their approach, and the company lost millions of dollars. Nearing the end of the year, I had to step in to try and salvage the client relationship. Unfortunately, it was not successful. In January, I had the difficult task of letting them go. I'd decided in mid-November but had chosen to wait because nothing good comes out of letting someone go during the holidays. There is no bottom line to justify that kind of disrespect.

When we met in January, I said, "We need to have a difficult conversation. If we look back at what happened and look at how we talked about the risk - well, the risk didn't pan out. I have to let you go."

Their response? "What took you so long?" They'd expected to get the boot during the holidays. Going back to our original conversation, they'd chosen to put their job on the line. Our talk on this day in January didn't come as a surprise.

It was a tough one, but it was clean and clear and expected, and that's because the original conversation had been clean and clear, outlining what would happen and spelling out the consequences. I hadn't said, "Do it my way." Nothing about that is empowering.

What is crucial and what you must have at all times as the foundation for any sort of conversation is respect. If respect is present, you will consider the message you are about to deliver. For me, the key piece is, "How would I want to hear this if it was delivered to me?"

Ideally, if communication is kept clear, clean, and respectful, there should be no surprises. If someone is surprised when they are let go, or if they receive a poor performance review, then intentional communication is badly lacking in the relationship.

If I have empowered you to own something, and if you have taken on that accountability, whether it's personal or professional, I want you to know the consequences before we leave the conversation. If you choose to own something, then you are accountable all the way. More importantly, you have to know the ramifications of what you choose to take on. We have to agree on expectations and consequences. At the heart of intentional communication is agreement.

This approach works with anyone, even children. Consider your child struggling with grades. "Can we agree that if your grades drop below a C, and you have not come to me for help, you will lose your gaming privileges?" And if they say, "I don't agree with that," continue to communicate. Why are grades important? What evidence do you have to back it up? And listen to them. You may find another avenue that works and that you can agree on. There is a difference between imposing a mandate on someone and inviting them to the table to participate.

My grandson's hockey coach gives a talk to the kids and parents at the start of each season. He says, "Parents, the probability of your children leaving here and getting a scholarship to a division two university is very low. The probability of them making it to the NHL is a fraction of that. Let's all set our expectations on what this is about – having fun."

You have to be open to ideas that don't align with yours. You have to listen, and not listen to placate or respond, but listen to truly understand. Pick any major city on a map. How many ways are there to get to the city? At least three and probably more. My route is not the only one to get me to the destination. The same goes for conversations. Staying in the mindset of *there are multiple ways to get to the end goal* will organically enhance conversations.

How you have conversations can have such a massive ripple effect, and you must start with respect. Respect in communication opens the door to better relationships. As head of a leadership team, I once worked with a leader who wanted to hire a job applicant. Based on what I'd read in their resume, I didn't agree. I considered it a high risk at best. I asked my team member, "Have you done your research? Do you know enough that you're willing to put your reputation on the line?

She paused, thought a minute, and said, "Let me get back to you."

When she came back, she said, "Absolutely."

We hired the person, and it was a great decision.

Afterward, she told me, "Through that experience, I now do all my research before bringing in a recommendation."

What does proper delivery of a conversation result in?

Learning, growth, and a feeling of right-ness.

If you're skeptical like me, by this time, you might be saying, "Sure, those are great examples of communication if you're in a nice, calm space, but not everyone is in that space."

No, they're not.

Back in 2007, I was running a small company, and we were doing exceptionally well. One of the requirements of our work was the pristine filing of documentation. We were working in a regulated environment. Even the slightest misfiling could result in an audit, which could jeopardize future business. I made the importance of meticulous filing clear to the staff, including why it was essential and the consequences if we messed up even slightly. I made suggestions and asked for input on how we could keep on top of it.

I thought I'd communicated the importance of meticulous filing, including why it was so crucial, but I continued noticing that the message and the associated actions were not in sync. I was beginning to wonder if I needed to speak a foreign language for the team to understand!

One day, I went into the filing room and noticed a critical mistake. My level of upset shot into the red zone. I had to address it. At the same time, I had to acknowledge my emotions. Clearly, my previous communication hadn't penetrated deeply enough. I brought the staff into the filing room. "I'm going to apologize now for how I'm about to talk to you," I said. "I am frustrated. I am disappointed, and I am downright angry. So I apologize now for yelling, or what you might perceive as yelling, or any other way this conversation is going to leave you feeling."

And then I let it rip.

When I finished, I apologized again. "If I've hurt anyone's feelings, that was not my intention, and I do apologize. I needed to get that out because my repeated, calm delivery and requests to stay on top of pristine filing have not been getting through."

Before I left, I recommended that they do an audit. My niece, who was one of the staff, told me afterward that everyone felt so bad, not because of what I'd said, but because they sensed they'd let me down.

We never had a filing issue again.

Communication is not always calm. Emotions can flare up, but your communication can still be clean, and you can prepare people for what is to come. It's okay to lose your shit, and it's your responsibility to share those things that made you lose your shit in the first place, but in a way that is anchored in grace and respect. As soon as the person you are communicating with goes into a stress response, your message will be lost. They won't hear you. Instead of listening, they'll be hunkering down behind a defensive wall. That is the brain's job – it's not a conscious choice.

Contrary to the old childhood refrain, words *will* hurt you, not just sticks and stones. Make sure your words will be received as you intend. "Are you open to some feedback?" is a respectful question. So is, "Can we agree?" or "Can we align?"

If my employee, who was willing to put their job on the line, had said, "I don't think I want to put my job at risk," I would have responded with, "Okay, then let's figure out another way to roll this out." They always had that option. I was always willing to work with them, and they knew that.

There is a difference between *talking at, talking to,* and *talking with.* I prefer to be talked with. I want both of us or all of us to participate. When you impose something on me, you're undermining any chance of me buying into what you're presenting. In communication with you, I'll assume you feel the same way.

Twenty or so years ago, I had an employee whom I could put in front of any customer. She could explain what we did perfectly. There was no one better. However, when it came to executing, she couldn't put theory into practice. We talked numerous times, discussing everything from being efficient to hitting timelines and performance, items she couldn't seem to grasp.

I finally had to make a choice on her future employment. First, though, I wanted to know what was going on and if there was anything more we could do. I started with the best place to begin: "Are you open to some feedback? Is this a good time?"

She said, "No."

Okay – that was fine.

She then gave me a list of all the personal and professional challenges that had absolutely brought her to her knees that day. She was right – this was not a good time. She didn't need one more piece of news she would clearly see as "bad."

"What's it about?" she asked.

I told her, "We need to talk about your knowledge of what we do and how it's not converting to execution effectively. We've talked about this before, so we know there are some gaps."

She nodded. "How about ten o'clock tomorrow morning?"

"Sounds great."

The next morning, she came into my office. She'd had eighteen hours to process the reason for the conversation, and she knew there would be no surprises because we'd touched on the subject before. I didn't have to say much. She agreed that she had execution issues and wondered if she was cut out for the job. "I don't know why," she said. "I really like the ideas behind all this."

I had a thought. "What about going into sales?" I asked.

She turned out to be one of the top inside salespeople we ever had.

I read an article recently by an HR professional saying that if you have to give negative feedback, particularly in a less-than-stellar performance review, you either deliver it and schedule a follow-up meeting that day to hear the rebuttal, or you send a document and schedule enough time for that person to process the information.

If we haven't built good communication behaviors along the way in our day-to-day interactions and conversations, then we will find ourselves in the unpleasant space of surprising people. Honestly, I don't like performance reviews. If you talk to your people regularly, why do you need them? There should be no surprises. How would you feel if you'd been working hard all year, thinking you're doing fine, and suddenly your boss slaps you with, "You're not doing a good job"?

Again, this is not limited to business dealings. Think about relationships. How often do you hear about people "just drifting apart?" Thinking back to some of my own failed relationships, especially early in my life, it's clear to me how the lack of communication, sometimes driven by a lack of trust, contributed to the end result. I can also say that because of the communication skills I've honed over the years, my current relationships are richer and more fulfilling.

If you are in that place of having to dump a surprise on someone for whatever reason, don't expect them to react well. Their stressors will fire up instantly, and they won't hear what you're saying. They may nod, but your words have no effect. You may have intentional communication down to an art form, but if you haven't asked if they're ready for feedback and you haven't given the person time to process information that is going to make them feel anything but glorious about themselves, all the techniques in the world won't work.

The way corporate America hands out termination notices these days leaves me furious. You get a random call and are told, "Sorry, you're out." Many people feel dumbfounded. They often had no warning – not a single sign that anything was wrong. What are you saying if you can't be upfront and honest with somebody? Why can't we have enough respect for people who've been working with us, sometimes for years, to say, "Hey, we need to talk about your employment."

If you, as an employer, immediately think, "Well, they may do something or steal something," then you haven't built a culture of trust. And I would add one other thing. If you're going to let someone go, before you talk to them and give them the reason, ask yourself why. And be honest about it. Why is it important to terminate this person? Be clear and clean with yourself. That's how you get to be clear and clean with others. I have a client who decided he needed to talk to a colleague about an issue that had left him feeling dismissed and disrespected. When I asked him a few weeks later if he'd talked to the colleague, he said, "No."

"Why not?" I asked.

"I guess it wasn't important." In this case, he avoided what would have turned out to be an unnecessary conversation for him.

Taking time to reflect and question your motives is time well spent.

We can never overlook the importance of intentional communication within ourselves or the significance of communication with others after imagining how we would feel if we were on the receiving end.

When we are delivering information, we need to be anchored in respect and facts, and then we need to listen to understand counterpoints, alternate ideas, or rebuttals. Our goal must be to come to an agreement or alignment on a strategy, a point of view, or a position that allows us to move forward.

It sounds so easy. It becomes easier with practice. Working at it is worth the time and effort simply because it's the right thing to do. That may be especially true if you face the challenge of adding different cultures into the communication mix. We'll tackle that subject next.

CHAPTER 6

Culture Wars

"We must disrupt to reinvent."

What is culture? Every definition source tends to agree with this one from Merriam-Webster: "The customary beliefs, social forms, and material traits of a racial, religious, or social group. Also, the set of shared attitudes, values, goals, and practices that characterizes an institution or organization."

When I refer to "culture," these are the definitions I have in mind. I have recently taken on a new position where the existing culture will very much factor into the initial choices I make. I'll be dealing not only with the organization's regional culture but also with the historic culture that has been built over many years. I'll even be dealing with buried cultures because the company, as it exists today, has been built on a foundation of numerous acquisitions but without deliberate thought and action to successfully integrate them into a unified culture.

Part of my job is to create a global culture that will work for everybody. I'm not new to the challenges I'll be presented with. One of the biggest is to get people to think about a way of working that will have aspects and expectations that may not be one hundred percent aligned with what they are historically used to.

People often operate from a position of learned behaviors.

"Why are you doing it that way?"

"We've always done it this way."

I tend to be a positive disruptor, which is simply about not doing "business as usual." We have to disrupt to reinvent, and my goal is to reinvent, which means taking the knowledge we have to date and making something new. If I'm inventing something, I'm solving a problem, starting from scratch; if I'm disrupting something, I'm mixing up the current status so I can reinvent it.

Reinvention is not an easy task, partly because of differing belief systems. You have a belief system that is largely driven by your family, your community, your tribe, your company, and probably your country, which is different from that of other families, communities, countries, and so on.

The concept of time is a perfect example. Much has been written about how different cultures view timeliness. Some countries put less value on "being on time" and more value on how we relate to one another when we're together.

The culture that countries like the United States, Germany, and others hold is that being on time is paramount. Promptness equates to respect for others' time. Which perspective is correct – promptness or a little leeway? When I told my story at the Landmark Forum, which perspective of my mother was correct? We have stereotypes about certain cultures that have been bandied about for so long because they are *generally* true. But are they factual? When you say you've bought a German-made car, people generally understand that you own a solid, well-made vehicle. Germany has a well-earned reputation for exercising a level of discipline and excellence in the goods they produce. Japan has earned a similar reputation. "American-made" probably gives many folks living in the U.S. and other countries a sense of confidence. It's a perception based on historical culture.

The country and community you grew up in likely influences whether you are a person who speaks your mind or whether you're more comfortable following orders and requests. These cultural behaviors have evolved over time.

In a large corporation with a diverse workforce, the challenge is to build a culture into which everyone can buy. The hardest thing to disrupt is the cultural values you grew up with. Those values are like muscle memory. You may not even identify them as cultural. *This is the way I'm familiar with, and it's the right way, and why doesn't everyone else believe what I do?* Your cultural beliefs are a lot like unconditional love for someone. Ask someone, "Why do you love this person?"

"Because I do." There may be reasons that partially explain why, but the only thing that really matters is You. Just. Do.

Going back to the cultural idea of "on time," I can't imagine being late for a meeting or an appointment. On the other hand, I have to tell a couple of my kids to arrive at our home thirty minutes earlier than the actual event just to make sure they get there on time (this is one example where I just *don't* get it). It may drive me crazy, but it's not a big enough hill for me to die on. Those hills exist, and we'll talk about them in the next chapter.

My children being on time is not one of them.

We are often faced with bringing hugely disparate cultures together. For some people, that may mean compromising on something important, and not everyone is willing to do that. If your job is to disrupt a company culture and reinvent it, or if you are leading any group of people who have been brought together for a common goal, you will meet resistance. How you handle it is critical to your success.

The conversation you start has to be anchored in dignity and respect. Ask them if they are open to change. Ask them, "What are you willing to consider that may be out of your comfort zone?" Give people the information they need. Why are we disrupting and reinventing? The "why" lies in the goal of having a harmonious—not standard—but harmonious group of individuals working together, possibly all over the world, who represent the organization's culture.

You may well run into cultures that are quite rigid or faith-based. Their precepts may be more important than the harmony you are trying to achieve. However, if you are in the space of having an open mindset, you can step back and ask yourself and them, "How can we harmonize around this?" Your goal is to find a way this person can be a part of this culture without sacrificing what is most important to them.

There is a difference between standardizing and harmonizing. If you want to standardize a choir, you can have them sing the same note in the same key. If you have the choir singing in harmony, they're not all singing the same note, but bringing those notes together creates a force multiplier that enhances the beauty of the music. When each singer brings their truest strength to the piece, the whole becomes greater than the sum of its parts. This phenomenon is particularly noticeable in *a cappella*. When I hear that kind of harmony, it can bring tears to my eyes. Why can't that concept work in cultural harmonization?

You have to determine what your non-negotiables are as they pertain to your culture. A Canadian friend told me recently about a law enacted in the province of Quebec that banned most public servants from wearing religious symbols at their places of work. These included hijabs, yarmulkes, and turbans. Some saw this as a reaction against Muslims. The Muslim community, in particular, protested vehemently. My friend asked me, "How do you deal with something like this?"

My response was no different from how I would respond to any impactful change. First, I would ask, "Why?" If it was a backlash against Muslims, as many people suspected, then I would say that unacceptable behavior should not result in stripping everybody of what is non-negotiable to them, in essence, condoning the unacceptable, egregious action of others. It is not for me to say, "You cannot wear your hijab or turban or yarmulke," because it's part of your religious freedom. But what I will say is that anyone who perpetrates a discriminatory act on anyone based on their religion will be terminated immediately.

Discrimination is non-negotiable for me. Disrespecting other people's belief systems is non-negotiable because it is diametrically opposed to a culture of respect. And when a few people behave poorly, it's simply wrong to punish everyone. This has a tremendous bearing on fairness. No matter the reason, whether it's discrimination or something else, punishing everyone for the indiscretions or outright wrongdoing of others is never right.

I'll never forget an incident in high school. It had such an impact, that I can relive it in an instant. The person slated for valedictorian shared my class in physics, where some people had cheated on an exam. I did not. The valedictorian did and was caught. Rather than give her a zero, the teacher, who stated he had heard others had cheated too, but had no proof, said that everyone had to take the exam again.

I stood, and said, "F**k you! I'm not taking it again. I shouldn't be punished because she got caught."

I stomped out and walked home, wiping away hot tears of anger. I burst through the front door and said to my mom, "I want out of that school."

Six weeks remained before graduation. I didn't care. My sense of justice and fairness had been so grossly violated that I was ready to forgo my graduation ceremony at the school where I had achieved so much.

My mom said, "If that's what you really want, that's what we'll do. But let's wait until your dad comes home."

My dad said, "No. We'll do this another way."

If my classmate had been given a zero as she should have, I would have been valedictorian Instead, I was salutatorian. As for my dad's "other way," it was rising above the injustice, using the platform I had as the salutatorian to share my message of honor and doing the right thing and walking off the stage knowing I had retained my level of dignity. Addressing bad behavior by punishing everyone didn't work for me then, and it doesn't now. As a national culture, we do that far too often.

I have a friend who has two Black sons who are both highly educated and talented. She has often written in her blog about the conversations she and her husband have had to have with their boys, conversations that would have been unnecessary if the boys had been White.

It is useful to examine your cultural beliefs, and to understand which are non-negotiable. Equally important is examining whether those non-negotiables are reasonable. Do your cultural beliefs fit into the culture you are living and working in? All cultures should not have to bend to your will. If you have firm beliefs that run counter to the environment or family or the company you are in, it is not their responsibility to bend to your will, but for you to determine how you can positively influence the culture you find yourself in. If you can't, then you may have to find a different situation where you fit better. If you can't respect and tolerate your situation or exist in it harmoniously, maybe it isn't right for you.

As I look ahead to taking up my new position where I'll introduce a new cultural norm, I understand I may well run into strong resistance from some individuals. When that happens, I want to know, "Is there any room for movement on that?"

If the answer is "Absolutely not," I might say, "Here's how I see that harmonizing. Would you agree?

If the answer is still "Absolutely not," then I'll say, "Let me help you find somewhere outside this organization that will be a better fit for you."

Bringing diverse people together in a company or department is not unlike two blended families coming together. There may be two adults with a couple of kids on each side, one a strict disciplinarian, while the other isn't even sure where their kids are as long as they're home for dinner. I hope that the parents will sit down and talk about this before they get married and commit to each other.

When my husband and I first met, he let himself be treated less than stellarly by his children, probably out of guilt and fear of losing that important relationship. I didn't like it, and I told him a story about moving in with my father when I was fourteen.

"My stepmother and I did not get along, almost coming to blows more than once (something I am not proud of, even to this day). One day, my father sat me down and said, Charlene, I love you very much. You are my daughter, and I will always love you. Polly is my wife, and she has chosen to live with me. There will come a time when you will be off creating your own life, and she will still be with me. Please don't put me in a position to choose because you're not going to like the choice."

I told my husband, "I can still hear that clear message to this day, and I'm not going to stand by and watch someone I love being mistreated. You can handle it, but if you don't, a point will come when I will handle it, and I cannot promise how I will do that. What I can promise is that you won't like it. And then, you're going to have to choose. Let's avoid getting to that point."

The great end to this story about my husband and his children is that they have realized that he is an amazing man and have accepted me, and even love me, as his life partner. One even refers to me as her "bonus mom." The family dynamic is strong and beautiful. We've harmonized.

Multicultural harmony is a powerful force. Walk through any Chinatown, Little Italy, Germantown, and so many more. Those places are magnets for every ethnicity. We seek that kind of harmony, and those neighborhoods are perfect examples of how different cultures can exist harmoniously and thrive.

I worked for a corporation once that included a large team in India, as well as other cultures. Our India team wished us a Merry Christmas and a Happy Hanukkah, while we wished them a Happy Diwali. I may not understand your culture as you may not understand mine, but we can recognize our differences and respect them. That is common courtesy, and it comes from a foundation of respect.

A corporation's most challenging cultural issues come with various inflection points in its growth. Companies tend to hit their first inflection point at fifty employees. The next comes between three and four hundred, and then at over one thousand. If someone isn't keeping their eye on what is going on, the culture begins to deteriorate or dilute.

When you have fifty or fewer employees, everyone's on board, ready to roll up their sleeves and get to work. We all want to be successful! We're all one big team! When you get to a hundred and fifty and more, you realize you need more infrastructure. This is the place where things could go wrong if you don't ensure you have the right leadership in place. It's also when you begin to think about efficiency and start to specialize. Bob can no longer be the person who answers the phone while also doing business development and overseeing accounts. You have to ask Bob which job he likes and put him there.

So you're growing, and you're getting it right and building a great culture, and suddenly your investor speaks up (or your shareholders if you're public). "You're not making enough money!"

Suddenly, your people-centric culture comes into conflict with a demand for more profits. I'm telling you they don't have to be in conflict. If they are, you're having the wrong conversations with your investors. If their focus is money, then they need to be educated about why the business actually works. You need to calibrate so that financial goals are in harmony with preserving the healthy culture on which the company was built.

It's important to note that culture will evolve. It has to evolve. Who you are as a ten-person company or a small nuclear family is different from a two-hundred-person company or a blended family. It's up to those in leadership roles to make sure the inevitable evolution does not depart from the foundation. The foundation is what makes the group or organization successful. Never lose that.

No matter how large the population in the corporation, congregation, or advocacy group is, it's essential to create and maintain a harmonious culture, which means we can have different opinions that can be harmonized peacefully – and that takes us right back to mindset. It is an absolute requirement that you have the internal, open space that allows new information to enter as well as the grace to give it airtime. Then, if you are honest with yourself and gather as much information as you can, you can make a fully informed choice. Your opinion and ideas may not change, or you may pivot.

If you keep an open mindset and a respectful space, the internal voice of anxiety and dismissiveness will dissipate. Those are the factors that drive hate. If I am dismissive of your opinion, I will become anxious when you speak because I already know I don't agree with you, and I'll argue against your opinion. With that negative mindset, you can *feel* the upset coming on. You begin to see the person who is speaking as the dreaded "other," and if you dig your heels in on that, you will not create harmony anywhere – not in your place of work, your family, or your community.

Hate and fear of the "other" is not a good hill to die on.

CHAPTER 7

A Hill to Die On

"The risk of dying on the hill brings lessons."

Why do so many people have a deep need to be "right"? Certainly, in some cultures, that need tends to be repressed, but it's widespread not only in Western civilization but also in societies across the globe. What do we gain by being right, especially if it is at the expense of a relationship? I believe we lose so much more than we gain.

We attach a value to being right, even if it's only on quiz shows. There's a rather excellent quote attributed (probably falsely) to both Mark Twain and Abraham Lincoln: "It's better to keep your mouth shut and appear stupid than open it and remove all doubt." I think it speaks directly to our desire to be right.

As a society, we have moved so far from facts to opinion that the argument about who is right has become more heated than ever. Since our last election in 2024, I keep hearing that the mainstream media has never been more irrelevant. We weren't listening to facts. We were hearing opinions on both sides of the aisle, and both sides dug in their heels harder and harder in an insatiable need to be right about their particular belief or opinion, a need so overpowering that they chose it as their hill to die on.

A hill to die on, for me, means that you have such profound belief in the topic, cause, or circumstance that you are willing to fight for it and quite possibly put your reputation and/or your relationships at risk. That's how deeply you believe in what you're fighting for. So, one would think our choices on which hills to die on would be mindful and not selected lightly. If only that were the case.

When you pick your hill, you are doing yourself a disservice if your judgment is clouded by the need to be right. If you take a step back into an open mindset, you can consider the fact that perhaps you're not right, or you're partially right, and the person whose opinion is different from yours may have a point. Remember, truth is not the same as facts.

As you build your ability to keep an open mindset, I believe you'll find that the number of hills you choose to die on diminishes.

Consider what the other person is saying, and then determine whether you agree or disagree or whether it's important enough to risk a relationship. Proving the wrongful thinking of my relative, whom I strongly disagree with on many subjects, is not a hill I plan to die on. First, who am I to say he's wrong? We both have opinions. I can't *definitely* say that either of us is right. If I stay open to listening to him, I may find something that piques my interest. I will learn nothing if I shut down and decide he's wrong and I'm right and that nothing can change that.

If you're going to risk everything, including your reputation, make sure it's for something profoundly worthwhile and that you are clear and grounded in your facts and your truth. Make sure your hill is fully in line with your values and beliefs, so much so that it's worth the risk of losing a relationship, a friendship, a job, or even a piece of yourself.

When the employee I mentioned in an earlier chapter said that they were willing to risk everything to carry out their idea and plan, they were fully aware of what they were doing. They had facts and data. They had done tremendous amounts of research. They felt confident about the risk they were taking, and they knew the consequences they would have to face if it didn't work out. I suspect if you were to ask them if they had regrets, they would probably say, "None."

I've died on more than one hill in my professional life. I will always take that ultimate risk when an organization's leadership morphs into a culture that is not employee-first. I will leave that company every time. When you put profits before people, you're directly challenging or trying to negate my value system. That is non-negotiable for me. I cannot and will not put profits before people.

That's where I draw a line in the sand.

But if and when dying on that hill goes wrong, as it did for my employee, what do you take away from that? What's next?

Dying on the hill is as important as living on it. If you risk everything to see the "right" thing done, as I did in high school when I refused to take a do-over test, what then? There is a price to pay. When my employee failed with his idea, they paid a price. Their personal life and health suffered, but one thing didn't – their reputation. Why not? Because before they climbed their hill, we had a fact-based, up-front dialogue that clearly outlined the consequences. We agreed on them.

I could have paid a big price when I walked out of my physics class with only six weeks to go before graduation. I was young and lucky to have my father and mom's support. However, I did not compromise or damage my integrity. Losing that would have been a much bigger price than sacrificing six weeks of school.

Today, if I took on a new position with a large corporation only to find that it violated my value of *people before profits*, I would pay a price for standing firm in my integrity. What is more important than that? I believe that as we get older, our tolerance for what we'll put up with diminishes. When we're younger, we tend to tolerate more in our professional and personal lives, even if we have to grit our teeth to do it because the necessity of bringing in a paycheck is bigger or being alone is scarier than the perceived security of the relationship.

In the end, it all comes back to my value system. If I don't stand for that, then I don't have integrity, and if there's only one hill to die on, I can't imagine a more important one.

Too often, I see people in a corporation, or even in a family, hold back or give up because they don't think they have the power to influence the direction the group is moving. They choose no hill to die on, the direct opposite of those who choose everything as a hill to die on. I want to tell the younger generation that they do have the power to influence, and to choose those causes carefully. It's all in how you do it. You don't effect change by yelling, "Change!" in someone's face.

It goes right back to the model for intentional communication. It's *how* you deliver your message. If I found myself in a company that focused only on the bottom line, I would figure out a way to speak my truth so that people would truly listen.

It should never be profits over people; it should be people driving profits.

Dying on my hill is a last resort. Before that, I would deliver my message in a way that would make people open and willing to hear it. I also have enough data to say confidently, "Yes, it works."

When all else fails, go ahead and take your stand. With a mature mindset of space and grace, you can carefully consider the risks, weigh the consequences, and walk forward with purpose and clarity.

CHAPTER 8

Space and Grace

"We are all perfectly flawed human beings."

Remember the safety talk on an airplane before it takes off? "If you're with someone who needs help with their oxygen mask, put yours on first, then give them a hand." For the same reason, practice giving yourself space and grace. The better you are at honoring yourself in your less-than-stellar moments, the more you'll have the capacity to be there for others.

If you're in one of those situations where your calm, peaceful mindset is abruptly overturned, give yourself the space and grace to simply be human and respond (but take care where and how you respond – we'll get to that shortly). Let yourself be fully and unreasonably emotional for as long as you need. Go ahead and throw soft-squishy things (safety first!), then remember to shut the box (more on this later), staying aware of the mindset you ultimately want to experience. Step out of your "emotional time out" without bringing along the judgments, assumptions, and suppositions that go along with your very human reaction.

We are perfectly flawed human beings who are not going to be the optimum version of ourselves every day – and that is perfectly okay.

My husband and I were staying at one of our favorite hotels in the fall of 2024, where we had been having challenges all weekend with the housekeeping and restaurant services. On two occasions we asked for the room to be cleaned. Although we were assured it would be handled, it wasn't. We ordered room service, which wasn't really room service as I had to go downstairs and pick it up, and the salad was so bad, it was inedible. Finally, when housekeeping cleaned the room, it was unacceptably done.

I was not happy – and I'm human. I grumbled to my husband, complained, and probably swore. I stewed on my emotions for a day or so, allowing them space to get out of my head. Then, I closed the box. The evening before we checked out, I went to the lobby to speak to the front desk representative to let them know that the future stay I had already booked was at risk because of the numerous missteps all weekend.

"Good evening. Will you check if our reservation in November is prepaid?"

He checked his computer. "Yes, three rooms, and they have been prepaid."

"That's unfortunate as I was considering canceling." I paused for a moment, then continued with a simple question, "Are you open to some feedback?"

The look on his face was conflicted – on one hand, it was the same look you'd expect on your own face if someone said, "We need to talk." You know that feeling. On the other hand, there was a distinct look of confusion – how many people *ask* before starting on a diatribe? After all, rants and complaints were what he was expecting. With a noticeable amount of uncertainty, he said, "Uh, sure."

I told him how happy we had been with the hotel in the past. Then, I calmly said, "I don't know what's going on now, but this is the worst hotel experience I've had in many years – and I travel a lot." I enumerated the specific instances when we were dissatisfied. Then I said, "I also want to commend your front desk staff because any time we called, they did everything they could, even bringing up towels themselves."

The manager's expression had altered considerably. "Thanks for the feedback," he said. "I'll make sure it gets to the right people. Also, I am the front desk supervisor, so it is nice to hear good things about my team." There was lots of pride in that young man's face.

"Thank you for listening," I said. "And I appreciate any help you can give us for improved service next time we're here."

When we left and got on the elevator, my husband shook his head. "I don't know how you do that."

"Do what?"

"You were very calm. You just laid out the facts and told him what you were unhappy with – and you did it all without getting upset or upsetting him!"

I nodded. "If I don't live, be, and do what I plan to write in my book, the book will be useless."

Being angry and combative would have been foolish. I presented my issues in a way that allowed the person receiving the feedback to hear it and genuinely take it in. We weren't on opposite sides of an argument – we were together on this. We both wanted the hotel to give excellent service.

I'd entered the conversation with a clear idea of what I wanted to achieve. However, before I'd done that, back in our hotel room, I'd given myself the space and grace to be fully human. Anyone watching would have seen my flaws.

Giving others space and grace is as important as giving it to yourself, and when you do give it to others, remember to pay it forward to yourself. Recently, a friend picked my husband and me up at the airport and I could see that she wasn't in a good mood.

"Do you want to talk to her?" my husband asked.

I was tired and not at my best. I said, "No. I don't have the patience for it right now."

A day later, we went to a hockey game with her, and when I had a chance, I asked, "How are you doing?"

"Okay."

"Are you sure?"

"Yes."

"What's wrong?"

She paused, swallowed, and said, "This is a tough time for me right now."

I had some idea of what was going on in her life, put my arms around her, and hugged her. If I'd tried to handle the issue the previous night, it would not have gone well. I'd needed space to take care of myself so I could give her the best of me.

Treating yourself with as much respect and kindness as you give to others is not always easy, particularly for people who are hard on themselves with a perfectionist mindset urging themselves to always be at their best. A perfectionist mindset is ultimately exhausting. A kinder way to go through life is to give ourselves and others the space to make an error, be wrong, and even have a good rant.

This is where my Time Box approach comes in. A Time Box is

the process where you recognize that all your raw emotions are at the surface. Your executive center is on a coffee break, and the visceral response you are about to have is not going to be pretty. As the person having the response, you are accountable for understanding how big it is. As the receiver of the response, your accountability is bigger. The person coming to you with their "emotion dump" is deeply vulnerable. They have to trust that they are sitting in a "box" with you, and whatever happens in the box stays in the box.

As the recipient, you are the bartender. Bartenders could write books on the stories they've heard. They don't. They are listeners with no agenda. They listen without judgment and without any need to inject their story or viewpoint. If you are the recipient of a person's open, raw emotions in that box, anything said is sacred, and your job is to listen—that's it—and then immediately forget. Nothing said in the box can ever come back to haunt the speaker.

If your kid is losing it because he got kicked off the varsity football team, you have to give him the space to vent. If every other word is the F-bomb, which may not be acceptable in the home, it's safe in the box. In the box, there are no repercussions and no retaliation. It is a circle of trust. As the recipient, you must have situational amnesia.

As the receiver, it's essential you begin your "box session" by asking, "How big is this to you? How much time do you need to let it all out?"

One day, one of my associates came into my office saying, "I just need to vent."

I asked, "How big is the problem? How much time do you want?"

"I don't know," she said."Fifteen minutes."

"Okay." I looked at my watch. "Go!"

She went. She was raw and real. Nothing about her epic rant was in alignment with her personal excellence in leadership. But when she finished, she took a deep breath and said, "I feel better."

I looked at my watch. "You've got seven minutes left." We both laughed.

She just had to get the stressors out to give herself enough space to start problem-solving. Her executive center was back from its coffee break, ready to get to work.

After they've had their visceral reaction, I tell people, "Now we're going to come out of the box and close the box. The box goes away. Poof! Now we're going to approach this from a consultative perspective."

When our feelings are given expression, we can look at the problem differently. What was your kid's problem? He got kicked off the varsity team. Why? His grades weren't keeping up. Okay. "Son, did you ask how you can get back on the team?"

"No."

"Okay, I can help you with that." Then, together, you can come up with a plan of action to solve the problem.

It sounds almost too simple, and in a way, it is. But a Time Box conversation won't work if you haven't built unwavering trust. And how do you do that? It goes right back to engaging in authentic, intentional communication that includes setting expectations and respectful delivery – all the basics. The Time Box will not work if the person doesn't feel comfortable being a completely raw individual with you.

I've been on the venting end, and I know what a physical relief it is. With all the emotion spilled out, I find myself breathing again, my shoulders dropping, and the muscles in my face relaxing. The first time I did this with someone I trusted, my feelings spilled out in tears. I'd had so much anxiety building up for so long that letting it all out, complete with tears, was cathartic. And it was safe. I knew that when I was done, the box would close and disappear. Poof!

One day, a colleague came back from a meeting, more upset than I'd ever seen her. She was hurt, angry, and dumbfounded. She felt that her character had been called into question. As she spilled it all out, and based on what she was telling me, I did not detect an attack on her character, so I just listened. What I thought about it didn't matter. What was important was that I was clear in how she received it.

"How much time do you need?" I asked.

"I'm going to need the whole weekend," she said.

It was that big – and understandably so if she thought that everything she stood for was being questioned.

The Time Box can be any size. It just can't be infinite. The box has to have sides. However, the longer you stay in the state of being upset, the harder it is to close the box.

The fact that my colleague needed the weekend was okay, but my husband and I were leaving on an Alaska cruise, which would mean quite a difference in time zones. I asked her, "Do I need to get up at 2 a.m. on Monday to send you a note to make sure you've closed your box?"

It turned out she didn't need the whole weekend. She and her family went to an amusement park, played, and had fun – and that was what she needed to be able to say, "It's time to close the box." After her visceral reaction to me, she dealt with her feelings by removing herself and allowing her subconscious mind to work through the issues. By Monday morning, she'd decided she didn't need to talk about it anymore.

She didn't even have to create a plan of action. What she needed was a change of perspective, allowing herself to consider that the events had not spoken to her character, or that the events and perceptions were not worth any more worry because she knew exactly who she was and that she was stronger than any unfounded chatter.

When you give yourself space and grace to be human, and when your problem-solving skills return, you have to go back to the trigger that set you off. There will be an event or series of events. When you close the box, you become the consultant. You look at the facts of the problem and present possible solutions.

This Time Box method is one of my *Hills to Die On*. I have yet to see it backfire. If you give people the space to be what they are "not supposed to be" because they are top-notch leaders, after all, they will actually become better leaders. When people tell me they put me on a pedestal or consider me a superhero, my immediate reaction is, "No – not me. I'm a real person. Yes, I want you to look at me as a beautiful human. I'm not some kind of mythical being."

We need to give people the space to know they don't have to be on it all the time and the grace to let them have their bad days and express their emotional responses without judgment. You must have situational amnesia. This method requires an unwavering level of trust and respect.

Some people don't have a bartender in their life. You may ask, "What about them?"

Here's my answer: I challenge everyone who looks at themselves as a leader to figure out how to become one. And do it now. That should be one of your key accountabilities. Any leader who thrives on the fact that people are afraid of them has nothing to be proud of.

In 2009, I was brought into a company to help clean it up. Part of that assignment was making the tough business decision of letting some people go. Despite all the communication skills I have and all the leadership qualities I'm proud of, I missed something because I heard that people were calling me "The Grim Reaper."

I was cut to the core. What had I missed? When I analyzed it, I realized I had failed to bring the entire team together to impart all the facts. I had told the leadership team, assuming they would pass the message along to their people. Because of what was going down within the company, the message should have come directly from me. I was making the decisions. Had I sat down with the whole group and told them the full extent of the situation—including what I was looking for and the kinds of choices I would have to make—they would not have been surprised. I learned a big lesson.

However, any leader who wears their team's fear of them as a badge of honor needs to rethink their approach. They will never get to the bartender stage. People will not come to talk to them.

In professional settings, the person working in the trenches, the individual contributor, is as much an adult as the leader. The organizational chart tells us there are different positions in the company and it may look like a hierarchy, but the bottom line is that what we're dealing with are two adults who should be able to have peer conversations.

It's not all on the leaders, either. As I said, you are an adult. If you enter into a conversation with a person with no judgment, predisposition, or conditions, no matter what their "rank" is, you can create a conversation. My daughter was a restaurant owner before she worked for a corporation. Why should she diminish those talents and become subservient? If that is to change, she must change it. That may be more difficult for some people who are in minority groups or have grown up in a family or society where they were undervalued. If you are one of those amazing people, I encourage you to seek your value – because you matter. Most of us operate in a system structure that rests on hierarchies, whether it's a church, a corporation, an organization, or even a family, and people tend to slot themselves into their roles. But does it have to be that way? When I'm in a leadership position, I print out the organizational chart and hang it upside down on my wall as my everyday reminder that the people at the top are the reason I have a job. I flip it to its "normal" position when a problem hits us. Then it's my job to protect those people working tirelessly every day. I am their shield.

Somewhere along the way, we've lost tolerance and respect for our differences. I believe that space and grace combined with Time Boxing is a way to start resurrecting some of our natural talents, such as the ability to engage in heartfelt conversations.

CHAPTER 9

The (Lost) Art of Conversation

"Critical thinking is a skill that has to be built. It is not exercised in an echo chamber."

L et's go to Merriam-Webster again. It defines conversation as an oral exchange of sentiments, observations, opinions, or ideas. Note the word "oral." Conversation does not include texting, emailing, or instant messaging.

I want to point out that conversation is not communication, which Merriam-Webster defines as "a process by which information is exchanged between individuals." Conversation goes far beyond data exchange.

I can remember the days before we had email. No, they weren't one hundred percent "good old days," but there's something about a voice and a face and a body in front of you. A person's gestures and expressions are so important to fully understanding what is being communicated, and they complement the conversation for a deeper understanding.

Until you are comfortable with the tools of intentional communication that are clear, grounded in respect, and based on fact, there is immense room for misinterpretation in a text or email. The voice, face, and body carry emotion and meaning that you can't get from a written message.

You know how much you can read into a person's eye roll or

crossed arms or complete lack of eye contact. That's why I call the art of conversation an activity. You are not an observer or reader. You are a participant.

Emailing me is like sending something to a black hole because we are flooded with spam, promotions, ads, and social media notifications. I can't be expected to look at all thirty thousand and twenty (and counting) unread emails in my Gmail account. I'd rather you "go retro" and pick up the phone. But what if you tell people to call and you're not available? Let it go to voicemail!

Talking to someone on the phone is active communication through conversation. You have to use words and listen to a response. Talking in person is active: again, you have to listen, and you also have to watch a person's face and body while being cognizant of yours. A genuine, active conversation is more than just words, but with the advent of technology we have reduced and even replaced the art to the point where, for some people, it appears to be entirely lost. Instead of conversations, we have emojis, icons, and ALL CAPS.

Conversation has devolved from activity to passivity. Technology has made us lazy.

That said, technology, including group chats, is amazing when used for the intended purpose of sharing information. However, sharing information is not a conversation. It is not an exchange of sentiments, observations, opinions, or ideas.

I recently had a group chat with my kids to give them my travel schedule, but when I need to have a conversation with them, particularly if the subject is sensitive, a text message or email will be my last resort. The misuse of technology to have a conversation is not fair

– not to my family, my colleagues, or my friends. We've all heard about people breaking up relationships or being fired by text messages. That's one hundred percent unacceptable. It shows complete disregard for another person's feelings. How self-centered must one be to shy away from a real conversation on a topic so impactful, rationalizing, "I don't like conflict" or "I'm too busy"? Impactful conversations, positive or negative, deserve to be conducted face-to-face. It's foundational in giving respect, and respect is the basis of great communication.

Passive communication is eroding our social accountability and human bond of respect. It also promotes unacceptable behavior. No one has the right to insult someone's character. Social media, which seems to have become the substitute for real conversations, is making it too easy to speak with hatred. And why do we do that? What are we accomplishing?

Do we feel right? Do we feel righteous? What did we gain? Yes, we have a fist-pumping moment of "I got him," but what are we getting in the long term? Are we becoming better persons? Do we have more self-respect? Is this type of hate-filled conversation what we hope to receive?

If you go to any social media platform and scroll down the comments on a post, you likely don't have to scroll far to find someone attacking the character of the person who posted. You may not like the person, but that doesn't give you the right to call them an unprintable name.

I have no objection to commenting on a behavior, but a person is not necessarily their behavior. "What you posted strikes me as rude" is very different from "You're a terrible, rude person." I can comment that these are the behaviors that lead me to not wanting to be in their presence. That's my truth – not a fact, just my particular truth. But I don't get to call them a derogatory name.

Why call people names? Why do people feel compelled to do that? I don't have the answer. Are they so miserable in their own existence that the only way to find any kind of gratification is to hurt others, perhaps in the way that they are hurt? Are these people representing their authentic selves, or is there an opportunity to let go of being right, opening up their mindset to receive other opinions and perhaps realize that it's not a hill worth dying on – perhaps a mindset reset?

I don't know.

Is hiding behind a keyboard the only safe way to express opinions?

What if we expressed our viewpoints with integrity instead? Maybe people would listen. What if people started an actual conversation? What if we came to the table with a mindset of respect, dignity, and openness? What if we approached a conversation with the intention of listening to others and trying to understand their point of view? We don't have to agree, and listening is a sign of respect. If I have space in my mindset to entertain new ideas, I can accept or reject them. It should be a *conversation* involving voices, faces, and real people.

You may disagree, but if you stay in the space of trust, respect, and dignity, you may learn something, or you may pivot, or you may just come away feeling good about yourself because you granted space to another person. And as you give that room and respect to another person, you may get it back as well.

Attacking someone's character or using inflammatory language will have the opposite results from what you may want. You'll shut people down. You won't learn. You won't grow. You'll stay in your silo or echo chamber. If you seek out only people who agree with you, if you embrace only groupthink, you won't expand your world, and you may lose the ability to empathize with others. We all want people to say, "Yes, you're right." But we expand our worldview by considering other viewpoints. As Steven Covey said, "Seek first to understand. Then to be understood."

Critical thinking is an ongoing exercise to tone and optimize your brain. We won't exercise it by staying in our echo chambers. Critical thinking is point-counterpoint. You can stay in your silo and be right, and have everyone agree that you're right, but where does that get you? Are you learning, evolving, or growing? What have you given up to be right?

We are pack animals who thrive in a community. (My heart goes out to the elderly who are far too isolated.) I want to see people make a deliberate effort to resist the urge to communicate passively and start actively making conversations. The phrase "making conversation" describes exactly what it is – something we create together. If we don't, we will continue to lose our ability to empathize with others. Online communication is not bad—not at all—but we've swung too far.

We need to relearn conversation. We need to teach, or maybe re-teach, it. I'm not sure what today's generation is learning about conversation. You can trace our ability to have a conversation from before technology, the early stages of technology, and today's reliance on technology. There was a time when you wrote a letter if you wanted to talk with someone, or you knocked on their door. You'd sit down over a cup of tea or coffee, and you talked, sometimes for hours. It was human interaction.

We need to resurrect that interaction. As technology has accelerated, we've become lazy. The book *Stolen Focus* by Johann Hari points out the connection between technology and the physiological impact on the brain. The development of our children's brains is being affected by the constant exposure to technology, and not necessarily in a good way.

If we are deep inside our devices, we are not conversing with other humans. You may think that one person—you—making a change can't possibly have a big enough effect to make a difference. Or you may well be the pebble, or dare I say rock, that sends a ripple out much farther than you thought possible.

CHAPTER 10

Rock and Ripple

"Cure the disease instead of treating the symptoms."

I magine dropping a pebble into a pond and noticing the little ripples that spread out. Now, imagine dropping a big rock into the same pond; notice the large waves it sends out. If you want to make meaningful, positive changes in your personal life, your workplace, or even just in your attitude, find the big rock that will create a big ripple effect.

Now, think of the rock as the root problem of issues you may be having. You can't solve the underlying problem (the rock) by trying to stop the ripples. Band-Aids are not a solution. You have to be an archeologist and dig for the biggest rock you can find. It's important to note that the "biggest" rock may not be defined by size or volume because sometimes, the biggest rocks seem quite small in size on the surface.

In business, we call it *root cause analysis*. Focus on the root problem, not the ancillary issues. If you solve the root cause, the secondary difficulties will often take care of themselves. Digging deep turns out to be a highly economical way of spending your time. That's important to me because anyone who knows me will tell you that I'm all about efficiency. I like to expend little effort for a big impact. My personal trainer, Danny, introduced me to kettlebells because they are the most efficient way to do both strength and cardiovascular exercise.

I'm also a results-driven person and a big fan of positive change. I want improvement by a big factor, not just little increments. When making any kind of change, you have to keep in mind the result you're after. If you find and handle that big root-cause rock, it may not solve every little issue your organization has, but it will make a significant difference. Auto mechanics do this all the time when they are fixing your vehicle. Their job is to look for the cause of that funny rattle, not to put duct tape on it. Doctors know this, too. Cure the underlying disease rather than just treating the symptoms. Unfortunately, we are often far too willing to take an Aspirin rather than look deeper for what is causing the headache.

Have we become too lazy to dig deeper? In so many aspects of our lives, we've moved from the effort and perseverance it takes to obtain long-term satisfaction to grasping for immediate gratification.

I'm afraid the age of wonder is disappearing. Every question we have can be answered by Google. How old is that actor on television? Google knows. There's no need to do any digging. Don't get me wrong, the advent of the ability to expedite comprehensive research is brilliant, but also risky if we don't keep our healthy skepticism well fed.

Rock and ripple isn't easy. If you want to get to the bottom of something, you have to dig, and you have to continue focusing on your excavation for some time. You can't stop once you're past the topsoil. You'll hit hard ground, tree roots, and small rocks on the way down. That's why knowing the result you want to achieve is so important. You have to know that the work is worth it.

If you want to create a beautiful garden in what is now a weedy patch of yard, you must dig out the weeds by the roots. That takes perseverance and willpower. You might have a fine-looking yard for a day or two if you just cut off the surface of the weeds, but they'll grow back. You need to dig deep to get them all and create lasting beauty.

Of course, I'd want to get deeper than just digging up weeds. Why are the weeds there? What caused the garden to become overgrown? Was my focus elsewhere? Did I just not care? Maybe I have to change my attitude. I may want to ask myself if the garden is really important to me. If it is, then digging up the weeds will pay off.

When we have problems in our relationships, we often can't see the rock because we're too busy dealing with ripples. Maybe I have a full-time job, and I get home and the children take up all my time, and at the end of the day, after doing the housework and a load of laundry, I fall into bed exhausted. Those are symptoms.

The rock is *why*. Why am I spending all my time on everything and everyone except my partner and me? How did this happen? Maybe I've allowed others' priorities to dictate my time rather than what I think is most important. Do I really have to enroll my kids in eighteen sports and activities?

The rock I dig up may not be pretty. I may have to admit something about myself I don't want to. Perhaps I'm addicted to work. Perhaps there are troubles in the relationship that are driving a lack of intimacy. Maybe I don't believe I'm worthy of self-care. But addressing the root cause of my dissatisfaction and tiredness will have a profound effect. If you're not willing to dig because you're afraid of what you might find, nothing will change. "My schedule is just too busy," is not a cause – it's a symptom.

In a company, the root cause of issues is often human error combined with the lack of a disciplined process and quality control. You can't modify a human, but you can change a process and alter the quality control component. Human error is different from human attitude. An attitude can be changed. Genuine errors occur simply because we are human. We have to be brutally honest with ourselves when we're digging into root causes. We must examine our part in it, especially if it involves interpersonal relationships.

One of my clients heads up a department of a large company with a culture that needs to be addressed. Unfortunately, he's in no position to do that. My question for him is, "What can you do inside your group?"

The big rock isn't only a root cause that has to be eradicated. We have the power to drop a rock of positive change that will send out ripples that will produce the results we are after.

I said to my client, "What if you drop the culture rock and take action on those things that are going to foster a healthy culture inside your department? I can promise you that your colleagues are going to notice. They're going to want to know what you're doing, and they're going to want to be part of that."

It starts with us. We are never helpless. Waiting for change to come from someone else, like a higher-up, is an excuse to do nothing. We can start a groundswell.

It's not always easy to admit to the rock or reconcile to it. The Rock and Ripple concept is a challenge to think deeper, be honest with others, and mostly with ourselves, and apply our efforts where the optimal, positive change can have a wide-reaching ripple effect.

Companies will often hire a consultant with the request, "I need you to do X." A high-performing consultant will ask a series of questions to probe deeper. Often, the consultant will say, "You don't need what you asked me for." They can then redirect the client to what they really need to address to get the result they want.

I was once hired to coach a manager at a company. Three months into the six-month agreement, they called to ask, "How's the coaching going?"

"Why do you ask?"

"We're not seeing an improvement."

"Hold on," I said. "What did you think this coaching was going to do?"

"Well, we're having some performance issues with them."

Had the people who were contracted to hire me asked the right questions, they would have told the company, "Coaching is not what you need. Leadership development and mentoring is what you need."

They were trying to treat a symptom. The person needed a skill they were missing. How can you enhance something you don't even have?

Rock and Ripple is about getting to the rock and making certain that you have indeed found the big one. We can use the three-year-old toddler methodology to get to the root cause. You know what that sounds like. Why? Well, because ... "Why? Well um...Why? Why? Why?"

You must be curious and willing to take the time to ask *why* over and over. Because information today is at our fingertips, this skill is not getting the attention it needs. Dig. Find the answer, and remember the role of the healthy skeptic. We need to be careful of the easy answer. Maybe it's the right one, but be skeptical. Keep digging. Trust your radar. It's amazing how often the "Aha!" bell goes off when we unearth the really big rock.

Some years ago, during COVID, I had to dig deeper than ever before to find the rock. I was in a crisis in my relationship, and because everything essentially shut down, I had a lot of time to reflect. I finally thought I'd pinpointed the source of my issues, but the longer I was isolated from the outside world, the clearer it became that I needed help with this one, and it wasn't until I saw a therapist that I unearthed the genuine rock. And no wonder I hadn't found it on my own! That particular rock was buried in the negative energy that had permeated my childhood. Looking back now, I don't know how I was able to bear it as a child and a young teen. My partner had inadvertently triggered that energy and the trauma that resulted from it.

The rock I finally found wasn't where I'd been looking. If you're trying to track down the source of issues in your personal life or at work, you have to be open to the idea that you may be digging in the wrong place. Give yourself the space and grace to understand that and that sometimes you may need help. There is nothing wrong with that.

The importance of the Rock and Ripple analogy is that you spend the time dissecting the problem so that you can find the biggest rock. Addressing it has a long-sustaining, profound impact. Unless you enjoy living in a state of insanity (doing the same thing over and over expecting different results), this work is necessary. It's okay if you don't find the biggest rock every time. It takes practice. The results are worth it.

CHAPTER 11

No Magic Bullet

"We need to get back to tolerance."

It starts with one: with you and me and us. When we reset our mindset, we create a groundswell.

It's important to remember that this mindset of tolerance, respect, and grace is not in a steady state. If you expect everyone to catch on with your new way of being, you will be disappointed. The world is populated with cynics and people who choose hate over love. They will not open this invitation, or if they do, they will RSVP with "regrets." That's okay. It's not about them. It's about us. Our tolerance may be tested, but isn't that what tolerance is for?

If we choose to accept this invitation, we will feel a sense of genuine emotional freedom down deep in our souls. It feels quiet and peaceful and balanced. It feels liberating. Imagine living your life with your mind open, free of sustained upset and anxiety.

When I started writing this book, I did not realize how important a quiet mind is. I have become more aware and have deliberately practiced what I "preach." I am a perfectly flawed human being, but I continue to practice. As I do, I find myself more and more in a state of being I can only describe as genuine emotional freedom.

Everything now is freeing. It's not ideal. It's not perfect. But it's freeing for me, and that's an okay place to be. It's not all butterflies and rainbows, but it's also not doom and gloom. This place of feeling free is real. It's not fluffy; it's solid. It's being present, not focusing on the past and all the things you "should have done and said," or on the future of "what ifs" and what horrors or joys it might bring. It's simply the peace of being here now.

When we simply "are," we allow space for openness and acceptance. I am fully aware that I have family, friends, and colleagues who cannot or will not do the work to reset their mindset and be in a space of genuine emotional freedom.

I hope you never use "My boss/friend/partner isn't there" as an excuse not to do the work yourself. Yes, it's hard work to get there, but it's worth it. It's easy to say, "This is just who I am," but it's in direct conflict with being authentic. It requires no work to stay where we are. It's a great excuse because you will rarely be challenged on it. But is it taking you where you want to go?

Please don't be deterred by the world around you. Don't let anyone, not even those you love, choose your path. As you build an open mindset and become more skilled in the art of intentional communication, coupled with effective conversation, external problems will begin to slide off you as though you were coated with Teflon.

I see my husband's stress every day when he comes home from work. I deal with it by looking for ways I can help. Ten years ago, I would likely not have taken that attitude. Being in a space of feeling genuine and present allows me to listen more intently. It allows me not to judge. It also allows me to help him think through what's best for him, and how cool is that?

My husband may not choose to answer the invitation in this book as quickly as I would like him to, but because I am in this mindset, I can help him and help our relationship thrive. Most importantly, I don't expect him to change. I have only one thing to say about expectations: you should have none. Part of having grace and space is not bringing your expectations into the interaction. It's hard to drop them, but they take up space. If you remove them, you have more room to listen and be there. As a result, the people who come to you will leave feeling as good or better than before the interaction.

We can be the bartender. It starts with one. And then the groundswell.

CHAPTER 12

The Invitation

"I invite you to start walking your path today."

This book is an invitation to you.

I invite you to believe you can be in a state of genuine emotional freedom and be okay. Depending on where you are in your life, the path you take will be unique to you. It may be a short one, or you may find yourself on a cross-country trip. Whatever your path is, I invite you to start walking it.

I invite you to be willing and deliberate in adjusting your mindset to accept the ideas I've laid out and to accept this path. We don't know what we'll discover along the way. It may be smooth, or it may be covered with roots, boulders, and walls – expected and unexpected barriers. If you accept the invitation to walk this path, your mindset should be ready for the good, the bad, and the ugly - those are fleeting moments, and you can learn from each one if you are open to new experiences.

I invite you to question what you are told, and what you see and hear. Don't take it all at face value. I invite you to be curious and to become a healthy skeptic. If your mind is open to ideas, everything becomes much clearer. Wear your healthy skepticism like a crown.

I invite you to establish clear, fact-based communication anchored in respect. Deliver the message like you're talking to the person you love the most. Honor the person and preserve your character.

I invite you to ensure that your audience is ready for your message. Don't be afraid to ask, "Are you open to some feedback?" Honor their character.

I invite you to recognize that alignment does not equal agreement. You can acknowledge and understand a point of view without concurring with it. This is the essence of a debate. Be debatable – it's the core of an open mindset: delivering the message, listening effectively, and acknowledging what is said.

I invite you to work toward cultural neutrality. By that I mean striving to respect multiple cultures and having the willingness to harmonize them. I invite you to create a cultural orchestra that harmonizes cultures from all different locales and situations to play beautiful music that is greater than the sum of its parts. The result of that kind of harmony is a place where we can have differing opinions, productive discussions, and respectful friendships.

I invite you to choose wisely in selecting which hill to die on. Every problem is not a hill.

I invite you to become a trusted and trusting bartender. What I have written in these pages only works if we can achieve a level of space and grace for ourselves as well as others. Open up the space to consider differing thoughts, opinions, and ideas, and the grace to listen to them, free of any judgments. When you do that, you become the bartender.

I invite you to try the Time Box approach. What do you have to lose ... or gain?

I invite you to go retro. Pick up the phone or, better yet, physically go and meet someone to talk to them. Go 3D.

I invite you to become an archaeologist. Dig to find the rock, the root problem of the small (or big) issues you are trying to deal with. You'll be glad you did.

Finally, I invite you to achieve a state of being that is okay regardless of what the world around you is doing. Don't give up on it. Work on it every day. It will catch on – I promise.

I hope you take me up on this invitation for the same reason you picked up or downloaded this book. I can share my story and tell you how well the practice I outlined here has worked for me. But that's my story. For you to take full advantage of this invitation, you must tell your own. If you're a skeptic, great. If you want to prove me wrong, terrific. You may well find something to challenge me with. Great!. As I said in the introduction, the reason I wrote this book is to help people. Through the work I've done over the last thirty years, I've learned that I seem to help people by telling my story.

I invite you to walk this path and write your story. I hope you start today.

Acknowledgments

Dave – for being my perpetual "beta test" for topics covered in this book, even, at times, unbeknownst to him.

Carmen and Marianne – for being the amazing ladies they are and for trusting me as a mentor, coach, and friend. Their willingness to try on my suppositions, views, and insights drove the framework for this book.

John M. – for simply saying on that fateful day in July 2024, "You should write a book." His simple phrase was the nudge that turned my "bucket list, one day" plan into action.

Goody – my partner, friend, and confidante as we navigated through this amazing experience. I'll be forever grateful to her for agreeing to be my angel writer.

About the Author

Charlene Dark is the Chief Operating Officer of Avania, an advisory and clinical development solutions partner to the MedTech industry, and the CEO of Summus Advisors, LLC, a leadership development and executive coaching services business specializing in the clinical research space. With over 30 years of experience in the industry, Charlene has been instrumental in driving innovation and excellence in clinical and MedTech operations research solutions.

Charlene holds a Bachelor of Science in Statistics from North Carolina State University and an MBA from the University of North Carolina at Chapel Hill. As a certified executive coach and executive leadership team coach, she has dedicated her career to empowering leaders and fostering growth within organizations.

Charlene is a connector of people, bringing together individuals of like and different minds, which has led to several valuable relationships not just with her but also amongst those she connects. Her commitment to personal development and community involvement is evident in her active participation in various initiatives.

In addition to her professional achievements, Charlene enjoys reading, doing DIY projects, attending Carolina Hurricanes hockey games, and spending time with friends and family. She has a blended family consisting of four children and eleven grandchildren.

Charlene authored this book in response to the encouragement and recommendations of many who believe her insights and experiences can add significant value to others. Through her writing, she aims to share her knowledge and inspire readers, inviting them to take a chance in disrupting and reinventing a mindset that provides a level of emotional freedom one cannot put into words.